Wishing all your days are Best Days

Always

Mark Keys

Laurie-Cell 949-531-1373

My BEST DAY SPORTS II

A Collection of responses from former &
current athletes and coaches

MARK KEYS

McCool Keys Press
5308 Neptune
Newport Beach, CA 92663

Quantity Sales. Special discounts are available on quantity purchases by corporations, associations, and others. For details, contact the "Special Sales Department" at the publisher's address above.

Printed in the United States of America.

Library of Congress Cataloging-in-Publication Data is available from the publisher.

ISBN 978-0-9897878-3-3

Cover design concept by Mark Keys & Erik Escher
Cover design art by Erik Escher; Escher Creativity, Inc.
eschercreativity@sbcglobal.net 949-400-5987

Trademark #87-014, 269. Class 16 Registration 5,143,668

ACKNOWLEDGEMENT

I would like to thank the following people for their support:

My wife, Laurie, my daughters Page and Megan, my mom, Virginia & Don Sheil, Glenell Parker for their love & support. Joan Parker for your kindness

And as always, the inspiration provided by the memory of David "Bucko" Shaw.

In addition, my appreciation to my supportive friends: Fred Howser & Family, Rod & Pam McNeill, Dick Butkus, Ivory Sully, Pat Thomas, Eric Dickerson, Bruce Arians, Nick Nunn & family, John Hamilton & Diane, Steve Virgen, Fred Lynn, Rick John, Billy Whitford, Ron & Wendy Lamerton & girls, Fred Pierce, Mike Wilsey, George & Lorene Kerr, Joe & Roberta McCarthy, Joseph & Marjorie McCarthy, Sam Dickerson, Cass Winsted, Blain Skinner, Diane & Jerry Tagami, Dave Wilcox, Roger Carlson, Mike Salmon, Sam Cunningham, Jon & Jane Arnett, Jim & Susan Ferguson, Jim & Cathie Helfrich and the entire Helfrich Family, Janet Curci, George, Sug & Casey Jones, Aaron Peirsol, Rick & Trish, Laird Hayes, and everyone who has helped me; especially Erik Escher-without his help the book wouldn't exist.0

Doctors Gerken, Gausewitz, Rhie, Bae, Ng, O'Carroll, Carlson and Katie, Bruss, Yaru- Pearl & Julia, Dobkins, Gordon, Shukla, Stringer, Wynn, Safman & Naomi Porter, and staff(s).

3

Also by Mark Keys

My
BEST
DAY
SERIES

AS SEEN ON **ESPN**

https://www.espn.com/video/clip/_/id/11924279

 Mybestday_MK   mybestdaybyMarkKeys

 markkeys0405

McCool Keys Press - Newport Beach

FORWARD

A good day, a bad day and a great day...such is the makeup of our lives. Mark Keys has had them all but manages to live the good days and the best days almost every day. This is a tribute to the love he shares with his family and the courage he shares with us all.

My Best Day is a wonderfully unique insight into what various sports personalities believe defines the highlight of their careers and sometimes even their lives. We all have great days and we all have memorable days...and then we have our "best day" and that is the moment that sits in our memory forever. It is that day that we greedily recall with anticipation and wonder. The days chronicled here will help you recall your own "best day."

FRED LYNN
Retired Baseball Player, Boston Red Sox, California Angels, Baltimore Orioles, Detroit Tigers, San Diego Padres

Game day, Baby!

-JAKE OLSON
USC Football Long Snapper

Today is my Best Day!

Yesterday is part of my memory.

Tomorrow is in the planning.

I pray that God helps guide me into tomorrow to enjoy a fullness of life and duty but today he has a hold of my hand as I see, hear and feel the present.
The breaths I took yesterday are gone but today treasured. To feel the soft fur of my pet and hear the birds start to sing as I watch the sun come up are only happening right now, today. Tomorrow may bring adjustments but today is in the moment. I just smelled breakfast cooking and heard the leaves rustle and saw my dog chase a squirrel. The peace I am experiencing right now is priceless. Yesterday was great and I pray tomorrow brings new joys but right now, today, I love what is happening. Today I can try to change some things that happened yesterday and plan for some for tomorrow but today I will try to carry out what I planned yesterday.

Today is my Best Day!!!

-JERRY KOOSMAN
MLB Player, NY Mets, Chicago White Sox, Philadelphia Phillies.
'69 Mets World Series Champion "Amazing Mets"

The Vancouver Olympics and winning gold in the downhill race in 2010. (I also won a bronze in the super-G.) After two previous Olympics, I achieved the ultimate goal.

-LINDSEY VONN

Olympic Gold & Bronze Medalist, 2010 Vancouver Games

My Hail Mary pass with no time left on the clock to beat the Detroit Lions on my 32nd Birthday was the most amazing game of my life. To be a part of that, to never give up, was my Best Day.

-AARON RODGERS
Quarterback, Green Bay Packers, 6X Pro Bowl, Super Bowl XLV and MVP, 2X NFL MVP

Every day is my Best Day

-JERRY WEST

NBA Hall of Fame, LA Lakers, 1972 NBA Championship, 1969 NBA MVP, 14X All-Star; Coach, LA Lakers; 7X NBA Champion, 2X NBA Executive of the Year

I've had a lot of good fortune in my lifetime, so there have been quite a few "Best Days" to consider, both on and off the golf course. Pressed to choose one, I guess it would be the day that I won the United States Amateur Championship. That was Saturday, August 28, 1954, the date of the final round of our country's most prestigious amateur tournament at the Country Club of Detroit.

I was just short of 25 years old at the time, working as a paint salesman in Cleveland with the welcome opportunity to play a lot of golf as part of the job. I had enjoyed a fairly successful career in my teen years and as a member of the Wake Forest College golf team. Then I spent three years in the Coast Guard, much of the time in Cleveland, where I was working when I qualified for that 1954 Amateur.

But, why was that August 28 my Best Day?

One obvious reason was the victory itself, but more importantly it convinced me that I had a future in professional golf, that my game was strong enough to compete successfully against the best pros in the world. A few months later, I turned pro and launched my career at the start of the 1955 season.

My first win on the PGA Tour came that year in the Canadian Open and I guess my decision was verified in subsequent seasons when I won 91 more tournaments, among them seven major championships.

The Amateur victory truly was the turning point of my career and life.

-ARNOLD PALMER

Hall of Fame, Professional Golfer, 4X Masters Champion, US Open Winner, 95 professional wins

The Ali Fights were my Best Days!

-JERRY QUARRY
Professional Boxer, 66 fights, 53 wins- 32 by knockouts

I was fortunate enough to have the greatest basketball coach, John Wooden, while attending UCLA. He influenced so much of my playing and my life. Starting my career under Coach was my Best Day.

I do have another pretty good Best Day, 1985 NBA Finals when The Lakers beat the Celtics was a sweet victory.

-KAREEM ABDUL-JABBAR

NBA Hall of Fame Center, Milwaukee Bucks, LA Lakers. 6X NBA Champion, 2X MVP NBA Finals, 19X NBA All Star, 6X NBA MVP

Mark, you are such an inspiration to us all! A career in athletics does take its toll on our bodies later in life—some far more severe than others. I am so sorry you have had to go through this…both of you.

Thank you for including me in your "what was your Best Day?" I love it when challenged to explore a part of myself and this did.

My immediate answer was today…thinking that would not be the answer anyone who want to hear. I spent the day mentally enjoying a review session of fond memories—I have three sons…each birth was definitely a most memorable moment—and many memories associated with them…searching highlights in my career…etc.

What was your best day? "Today" is still my answer. I carry so much gratitude for the life I have been allowed to live. I have been blessed with the ability to choose how I live each day. My life is filled with cherished friends and family who somehow manage to love me unconditionally. My parents encourage my love for sports throughout my life—when it was not a popular choice for girls. I am still able to exercise. I have always had a roof over my head and plenty of good food on the table. I love my job. I have been blessed with marvelous young women to coach, first rate colleagues and the ability in athletics to travel. I can live as a free

woman and person each and every day with choices because of others who have fought for my freedom. Of course, I have bad times of seemingly unbearable sadness and challenge. Those times provided an opportunity for tears, growth, learning and later the realization of hope. The joyful moments have been many. People have been very tolerant and forgiving of my mistakes. Each experience has created the person I am today. Today is the best day in my life…if you asked me yesterday or tomorrow…my answer will be today. I am blessed. Thank you for giving me an occasion to appreciate all that life has given me.

-JODIE BURTON
Claremont-Mudd-Scripps Basketball and Golf Coach

I cannot think of any truly good excuse to give you regarding a reply to your request for my Best Day. For one, I originally thought it was to be quite an extensive form of expression-only after seeing the book you gave me did I realize I was over-thinking the whole thing. But perhaps even more pertinent was, or has been, the notion that I felt I wasn't going to give either you or my stories any justice with where my mind was, or has been. Quite silly, really, and for that I want to say how much I appreciate your patience and kindness at what was likely a frustrating conundrum.

I think what you do is special, and it is my pleasure to add to your collection. Thank you for being so great along the way.

1) I think many would expect me to say that my best days were atop the podium at the Olympics or something of the sort. And, to be sure, those days hold a special place in my heart where few other days like it reside. Yet that feels too easy. But swimming gave me something, and it's an ability to feel comfortable in the water. I'm not sure many days have topped the swim I took with my dog, Judo, in front of my house in the winter or, when we were both face to face with a gray whale only ten feet from us. My dog paid little attention it seemed; but I could immediately feel the water moving around me as the whale was trying to navigate in shallow water. It looked at me as it picked its head out of the water, and it stayed there, and I didn't move for what seemed like

an eternity. I thought, right then, that this was why I swim.

2) It was always nice to win individually, but I found little joy that was greater than watching those I cared about accomplish a dream of theirs. One such story reaches back to the 2000 Olympic Trials. I was aiming to make my first team. My best friend at the time, Gabrielle Rose, was aiming to make her first US Olympic Team, after having qualified for Brazil four years earlier.

I saw her barely make the top 16, and then barely made the top 8 for finals, barely keeping it together for both. In the finals, however, she was on fire. From an outside lane, she finished second, and I can rarely remember feeling so proud and elated for anyone else, let alone myself. That showed me the joy to be found in such close relationships under extreme circumstances

3) I've experienced few days like it...I had just completed the Olympic Games in 2004, and remember sitting in the press room for the final interviews after my last race, and I felt a unique kind of euphoria come over me. I had just won three gold medals, or all of my races, in the same Olympic Games. I was appropriately asked,

"well, what comes next?" by an inquisitive reporter. All my gut felt like saying was, "I haven't the slightest idea" and that felt good. Why it felt good, was because I realized right then and there that I had accomplished everything I had set out for myself when I was just a child, over a decade prior. For the first time ever in my life, I can remember the feeling of having no more goals. A true sense of accomplishment washed over me…I had nowhere to go. And it felt oh-so-good. My eventual response was something along the lines of, "I'm going to let this feeling sink in, and I'm not going to set anymore goals for some time." It was then I learned the power of intrinsic fulfillment.

-AARON PEIRSOL

Olympic Swimmer, 2000 Sydney Games 1 Silver, 2004 Athens Games 3 Gold Medals, 2008 Beijing Games 1 Silver & 2 Gold Medals, Men's World Record Holder100 X Medley

When I was a kid playing pick-up games in the neighborhood, or whether I was playing by myself, I would always pretend I was playing in a big game. I would make up the circumstances or the situation and would create my own world. "He fakes, he turns, he shoots, and scores the winning bucket as the clock ticks down 5... 4... 3... 2...1." or.." It's a long hard drive into centerfield…Bleier is back against the wall he leaps and one-hand's it to end the inning." In the background I could hear the crowds cheering and people shouting congratulations, for at that moment you become the hero.

We all want to be heroes in some fashion and its only human nature to dream. Dreams create hope and hope fuels reality. Sometimes those dreams come true, sometimes they don't. Sometimes they become disguised in sheep's clothing.

My Best Day in Pro Football didn't come in a Super Bowl or playoff game or even a big game. It happened to come in my last game at Three Rivers Stadium. It was 1980, we were the defending Super Bowl Champions, and I had announced my retirement. It was Rocky Bleier Day, the game was against the KC Chiefs and with an 8-7 record the only place we were going was home.

It was a typical winter overcast day in December and the crowd was less than enthusiastic. They became less enthusiastic as we struggled to put 14 points on the board and then became silent when K.C. scored to take a 16 to 14 lead in the closing minutes of the game. We got the ball back on the 20-yard line and had to move it 80 yards to score. The way we were playing I don't know if we could have scored if the ball was on the 8-yard line.

We all believed there was nothing we could do until Bradshaw came in from the sidelines. He stuck his head in the huddle and said "Come on guys let's make something happen". Unconsciously something took over. You can call it pride, or that winning spirit, or stubbornness, but it was like the old war horse in his last charge to victory.

We started to move the ball. With runs by Franco and short passes to Swann and Stallworth we advanced steadily. Then a big catch by Calvin Sweeney brought us up to the 45-yard line and another by our tight end Benny Cunningham took the ball over the fifty down to the 44 yard line in plus territory. All of a sudden you could hear pockets of fans coming alive chanting "offense'' "offense" 'offense''.

With a time out and two minutes left on the clock the momentum started to change. At that moment Bradshaw decided to give me the ball six times in a row. He doesn't give me the ball six times in a game, but at the age of 35, beat to hell, he decides to give me the ball six times in a row.

With the clock ticking away I ran off tackle for six yards. Then I ran up the middle for four more. A quick pitch around the left end netted five, and a quick screen in the opposite direction got us another first down. Two quick-traps got us six more and as I was trying to catch my breath I could hear those pockets of chants changing from "Offense" ... "Offense" to "Bleier"… "Bleier"…. and soon there were 58,000 fans were screaming my name.

Bradshaw connected with Cunningham one more time to take the ball down to the 11th yard line and with 29 seconds left on the clock Terry called an off-tackle trap to the left side. We broke the huddle ... The ball was snapped and the right guard pulled to his left, I was behind him and the clock was moving 28...27... 26...With a tremendous block by the pulling guard and the left side of the line crushing their opponents, a hole opened up. It was the biggest hole I ever saw.

The clock was ticking 25... 24... 23... I turned into the hole and immediately got hit by the scraping middle linebacker, kept my feet as the clock ticked to 22...21... 20...

Ten black jersey's pushing me to the goal line ... 19...18... A safety came up to make the tackle I left my feet he left his... now two bodies hurling at one another... 17...16..We collide ... 15..14.....and I came down ...with the ball.... to cross the goal line.... to win the game. A dream came true. I scored the winning touchdown and as I was congratulated by my teammates, I could still hear the fans shouting my name and then it was over.

As exciting as that moment was, I also learned a lesson. Your dreams and wishes may come true but not necessarily always in the manner one would like. That doesn't mean they are not important, for all dreams are important. Of course, I would have loved to have been on the receiving end of the Immaculate Reception, but I wasn't. That play belongs to Franco Harris. But on the other hand, Franco didn't score a winning touchdown the last time he carried a football at Three Rivers Stadium either. Dreams are just a matter of degrees.

ROCKY BLEIER

NFL Pro Football Player; Pittsburgh Steeler, 4X Super Bowl Champion; Purple Heart & Bronze Star- Vietnam War

I had a great career, and they were all good days. I was lucky, I was always on a team that was competitive. All good days and very little bad days in all my seasons. The only bad year I had was my last season, playing for the Rams in 1982. It was an abbreviated season, with only 7 games, and I did not play. I have always look forward to football and anything to do with football. I never looked back, but I was always pleased with my seasons- no regrets. The only regret was not winning a super bowl; but that wasn't my fault or anyone's fault-or all of our faults-it takes the whole team to win. I had a great, long career and I am content.

-RON YARY

NFL Offensive Tackle, Minnesota Vikings, Los Angeles Rams, Hall of Fame, 7X Pro Bowler, 3X NFC Championship, NFL 1970's All Decade Team

My Best Day was May 3rd, 1977, I was at Texas A&M. Earlier that year in March, I wrote a letter to Coach Tom Landry, Dallas Cowboys and Texas Schramm, the Dallas Cowboy's owner. I asked them to please draft me. I was a huge Cowboy fan, being from Texas. The Cowboys sent me a huge box of swag-Cowboy shirts, sweats, hats, jackets, you name it. I was so happy! I thanked the Lord I was going to be a Dallas Cowboy; I had been a fan since I was 5. Then draft day came, after not being able to sleep the night before. I waited for the call from the Cowboys, I thought I had it after how I told them how much I loved them. Not to brag, but at Texas A&M I was a big deal, and All-American safety. I thought the Cowboys would like me for sure; I had the juice and they loved me. I expected the 214 area code from Dallas, but when the phone rang it was from 415 area code. I knew it was not Dallas, it was the Raiders! I was dressed in Dallas Silver and Blue, I damn near fainted when I was told that I was drafted by the Super Bowl XI Champions, the Raiders. I had to get off the phone, I started crying. I thought it was a mistake. I was crushed…and they were not happy tears. But, fast-forward a decade later and I thank the Lord for the phone call from 415 and the Raiders. I am a 2X Super Bowl Champion. No defensive back that played a strong safety from Texas A&M converted to cornerback-it was not logical; but I did it! I am thankful for Coach John Madden who drafted me, and all the other coaches like Willie Brown, for my Best Days.

-LESTER HAYES

NFL Corner Back, Los Angeles Raiders, 2X Super Bowl Champion, 5X Pro Bowler, Defensive Player of the Year 1980

1. Each day I finished all education levels- elementary, high school, college, graduate school. Emerging from WWII in good health. Marrying my wife, Jean.
2. The birth of each of our five children.
3. Our 50th wedding anniversary.

-JACK RAMSAY

Hall of Fame, NBA, Coach; Philadelphia 76ers, Portland Trail Blazers, Indiana Pacers NBA Championship - Portland Trailblazers 1977

My greatest moment was when I went to Arizona Western Junior College and I signed a letter of intent to go to Utah. We were 9-2 and we played a bowl game against Henderson Junior College in Las Vegas; which we won. Afterward two coaches from USC approached me, Craig Fertig and the linebacker coach. They called me when they got back to USC and told me they couldn't talk to me anymore because they found out I signed a national letter of intent. I was obligated to go to Utah. I called my mom & dad and said that I had to go to Utah as a junior because I signed the letter of intent, and the only way to get out of it would be if Utah fired their head coach. Utah was hosting ASU for a final NCAA game; but when the NCAA found out Utah was watering down their field before the game, the Utah coach was fired. I was now able to go play at USC! While at USC, we had a famed defensive team called "The Wild Bunch" and we went undefeated...playing UCLA in the final game. The 5 of us on the Wild Bunch got together five days before the game, and we vowed to stop their all-time leading rusher break the UCLA record. We stopped him, and I had a great hit in the 3rd quarter on him where the fans went crazy and my teammates went crazy. That play by me was the last thing he remembered, and it motivated my teammates to win. We all loved each other, and I think that is why we were so successful. That was my greatest moment at USC.

-CHARLIE WEAVER

USC All-American Defensive End, "The Wild Bunch"; Detroit Lions, Washington Redskins, 2nd Round Draft Choice Defensive Linebacker

My Best Days were many as a LA Laker, but the best was when I learned I had been traded to LA from the Detroit Pistons in 1964. Not only was I going back where I was born, but to a Championship team and playing with Jerry West and Elgin Baylor-two former college players I had played against in NCAA Finals…and Jerry was a teammate in the Olympics in Rome.

What a joy to play with a great team. I Roomed with Jerry West and played for a great coach, Fred Schaus.

Great memories and many "My Best Days"

-DARRELL IMHOFF

NBA Center, NY Nicks, Detroit Pistons, LA Lakers, Portland Trailblazers, 1967 NBA All-Star

I was nervous as I'd ever been. I've jumped out of airplanes, swam with sharks, climbed the Great Wall of China, ran with the bulls in Pamplona, been arrested- a *few* times—and recently told I have months to live. But as I stood in the dugout waiting to be introduced, I could actually see my heart beating through my blue dress shirt underneath my all-white linen suit. My fingertips were so clammy, they left sweat marks on the balls I used for my warm-up pitches, and I was rocking back and forth on my feet when Cubs manager Joe Maddon, who was to present me with a personalized Cubbies jersey to my pitch, walk up to me and lightened the mood with a little banter. As I looked around at the 40,000 plus Cub fans in sold-out Wrigley Field, I realized this team, this place, was the timepiece by which I could measure my whole life.

Almost all of my childhood birthdays were spent here, and in the weeks leading up, classmates would try to curry favor with me—bribing me with baseball cards and their lunch snacks- knowing that an invitation to Wrigley hung in the balance. We would arrive early enough to watch my idol, Ernie Banks, take batting practice, and I would marvel at his quick hands; his phenomenal balance; the way he loaded up his lower half and swayed his legs to drive the ball. The highlight of my youth was, as an eleven year old, winning a cub sponsored hitting contest, and getting to shake the hand of Mr. Cub himself. The picture of the two of us from that occasion remains one of my most treasured sports relics.

In high school, my friends and I would take the train from Geneva Station depot closest to my hometown of Batavia, into

29

Chicago for games, my parents even giving me their blessing to play hooky from school once in a while to catch a Cubs matinee, as all Cub home games back than were afternoon games. (I nearly always got away with it. Nearly. One time, my high school coach caught me on TV as I was catching a foul ball. Though come to think of it, why was Coach Tom MacMahon watching the game?)

My decision to attend Northwestern University in Evanston near Chicago instead of accepting an appointment to West Point, was tipped by the fact that I wanted to escape on the "L" train to Wrigley at will. I exacted my plan by choosing morning classes just in case I heard the call of the ivy, which I often did.

At the end of the Cubs' 1972 season, my classmate Dan DeWitt (who we called "Dimmer") and I hopped on the train to catch the Cubbies season finale. We scored tickets on the third base side, right behind the field tarp just beyond the dugout. I had it in my mind that at some point during the game, I was going to run onto the field, to experience, if only for a fleeting moment, the Wrigley grass under my feet. As soon as the Cubs closed things out in the top of the ninth inning, I blurted out, "Let's Go!" Without waiting to see if Dimmer was on board, I sprinted across the third base line and onto the infield as bewildered Cub players stood by, I like to think, amused. I touched second base and then ran towards first, by now in hot pursuit by Chicago police officers. I made it to first base and kept running, not towards home but rather towards the stands. I lunged over the fence on the first-base line as thousands of fans stood and cheered. As I raced up the bleacher steps, I noticed Dimmer right behind me. We ran down the ramp at Sheffield and

Addison Streets, with the officers still some thirty yards behind us. I thought we would make it. What I didn't know was that the officers had radioed ahead for security to close down the exit gates and Dimmer and I were quickly in custody, handcuffed together. They walked us back up the ramp, down the stands, and, unbelievably, across the field towards the holding cells.

"We get to do this twice" I said to Dimmer with a smile. And here I was, some 44 years later, about to walk on the same grass but this time, my senses took in everything—the freshness of the grass, the evening breeze, the sunset rays enhanced by the lights installed in 1988. I thought about all that has happened in my life since I sprinted onto the field in 1972, especially as it relates to my family, all of whom stood on the field behind home plate. There was my bride of fourteen years, Stacy, full of splendor and life and my heaven on earth. Next to her stood my oldest child, Kacy, a thirty-something NBA blogger and her sister, Krista, a 24 year-old Tampa resident and the most emotional of my children. To Krista's right was my oldest son, Craig Jr., the reason why I am still alive today. And there were my youngest children, Riley and Ryan, adorned in Cubs paraphernalia, looking on in amazement.

And now ladies and gentlemen, please welcome NBA reporter and Chicagoland native, Craig Sager.

Maddon insisted that I remove my suit jacket and pull the jersey over my head, which I eagerly agreed to do and then walked on the pitcher's mound. At another time in my life, I would have sprinted out of the dugout, full of Ernie Banks "Lets play two" attitude, but the weakness in my legs and my struggles with balance kept me to a walk, so I made the most of the moment by waving to the crowd like a politician.

Throwing out the first pitch at a Cubs game was a moment that I had never envisioned and a moment I had been preparing for, for four weeks, after I received the invitation. My preparation started with throwing a tennis ball with my son, Ryan, as my strength had been zapped by rounds of chemotherapy. But every day, I focused on getting ready for that first pitch and by the time I arrived in Chicago on May 31st, I was ready.

Cubs first baseman Anthony Rizzo, himself a cancer survivor, got down in a catcher's stance, punched his mitt a few times and gave me the nod. I put my right foot on the rubber on the mound and cocked my right arm back. The crowd seemed to go silent as the ball left my hand...

Funny how life comes full circle when you aren't looking. So much of my life has revolved around the world of sports, witnessing some of the greatest moments and players in the game. One of the greatest things about sports is that there is always tomorrow or next week or even next season. You gotta have hope.

Every year since 1981, I have placed a bet on the Chicago Cubs to win the World Series---that's thirty-five years of losing bets. In December 2015 while vacationing in the Bahamas, I put down $1000 for the Cubs to do it this year. You gotta think positive.

-CRAIG SAGER
Sports Reporter

Whether you are a college football player or coach you always hope you have the opportunity to compete in a Rose Bowl. On January 2nd, 2017 I had the good fortune to be a part of the Granddaddy of them all. What made it even more special was the men that I was surrounded by. It was a group of players, coaches, and staff that had fought through the adversity of a 1-3 start and truly came together as a family and a brotherhood. Together we were able to make one of the more special memories of our lives with a dramatic 52-49 victory over Penn State. To have the opportunity to represent the University of Southern California and the Trojan Family in that game was truly the honor of my life. To watch the confetti fall, view the sheer joy of our team, hug my family on that field, and hoist USC's 25th Rose Bowl trophy is a moment I will never forget and why it is my Best Day.

Thanks for the opportunity. Fight On!

-CLAY HELTON

USC Head Football Coach, 2015 Pac-12 South Division winner

Getting my contract extension (in 2016) was absolutely the Best Day of my life.

-CHUCK PAGANO

NFL Assistant Coach Baltimore Ravens,
Cleveland Browns, Head Coach, Indianapolis Colts

Very simply, my Best Day at the University of Miami was when my oldest daughter, Coral, graduated there three years ago on a full academic scholarship.

I had some big moments at University of Miami: I started against Bear Bryant in Alabama & Tuscaloosa, played against Woody Hayes in the Big Horseshoe, I was able to play in the Golden Dome against Notre Dame but nothing compares to watching your daughter walk down the aisle at graduation with a big smile.

-PAT MILLICAN
Football Player, University of Miami Football

I have been fortunate enough to have had many great moments. Two stand out...the first being the 1955 USC vs. Notre Dame game. We were heavy underdogs and I was fortunate to score 28 points (a record) and we beat them handily. A tie with that would be the 300 plus yardage game I had against the Chicago Bears when I was with the L.A. Rams. We broke an 11-game losing streak against them. These were both second to the day I realized there was really a God!

-JON ARNETT
NFL Player, Los Angeles Rams,
Chicago Bears, 5X Pro Bowler

Best Day of this season was Selection Sunday. I loved seeing the smiles and hearing the cheers of our players, having worked so hard to reach the goal they had set for themselves.

-MIKE BREY

Head Basketball Coach, University of Notre Dame,
Sports Illustrated National Coach of the Year, 2011

It was hard to pick my best day. Every day was a best day. Getting drafted by the NFL was a best day after not being a starter at Ohio State. Playing with Walter Payton was a best day. Leading the team in tackles as a rookie was a best day. Getting recently picked as one of the all-time top 100 players in Bears history was a best day. Being a coach in the NFL was a best day.

My best day in the NFL was the day I played on Monday Night Football against the Los Angeles Rams. It was 1977 and I was in my third year with the Chicago Bears. I was injured in the final exhibition game of the 1977 preseason. I partially tore my ACL ligament when I made a tackle and landed on the metallic yard marker on the sideline. I was placed on injured reserve for three games as I was rehabilitating my right knee. Based on my recovery, I was scheduled to return against the Rams on Monday Night Football. I worked very hard with stretching and lifting weights to strengthen my right knee. I watched video on the Los Angeles Rams to familiarize myself with the pass routes and running plays they used frequently. This game was going to be special. The quarterback for the Rams was my high school hero. The Rams quarterback was Joe Namath. I played quarterback in high school in Pennsylvania similar to Joe Namath. He grew up in a suburb of Pittsburgh similar to my situation. Joe was a star on the field and a television star off the field. Those 3 weeks of waiting to return were unbearable. I realized how much I enjoyed playing football. The Monday Night game week finally arrived. I was ready to get started. I felt healthy and was anxious to return. The week went by quickly as I returned to a normal schedule. Seeing Joe Namath on the film was surreal. I was going to compete against my hero. The Chicago Bear's record going into the game was 1 win and 2 losses. The Rams record was 2 wins and a loss. This was going to be a big game with the entire country watching the game. Maybe with our record and young roster the Rams would overlook the Bears. I could not believe how fast the week went by. Before I knew it, we were in the locker room at Soldier Field. Soldier Field was loud in pre-game and deafening when the game started. The game was back and forth. Every time the Bears scored, Joe Namath would lead the Rams back for another score. I was involved in many big plays. Many of these plays had an impact on the game. I had two interceptions and multiple tackles during the game. The final score was Chicago Bears 24 and Los Angeles Rams 23. The game was exciting until the final possession of the game when the Rams were stopped at midfield. After the game, I was able to have a short conversation with Joe Namath as he walked off the field. Just three years earlier, I was playing on special teams and backing up the starting defensive safeties at Ohio State University. Now, I am the starting free safety for the Chicago Bears and I just talked to my football hero. I just played on Monday Night Football and I am living a dream. If you believe it, you can achieve it.

-DOUG PLANK

Safety; Chicago Bears, Coach; Atlanta Falcons, New York Jets, 2X AFL Coach of the Year

To me every day is my Best Day. Of course, there have been days that are especially best. My family and friends, who, each and every day, provide me with all the love, understanding and encouragement I need to be successful. Of course, there are also those days in the NFL when your team has played an outstanding game and won. This is another Best Day.

-

WADE PHILLIPS

Defensive Coordinator; San Diego Chargers;
Former Head Football Coach, Buffalo Bills, Head Defensive
Coordinator, Denver Broncos Super Bowl Champions,
LA Rams; 2018 NFC Champion

Looking back in my life there has been so many days that could have been my best day of surfing. Bigger waves, amazing friends, new surf spots, better surfing, better conditions. You could go on and on about so many amazing days. There is one day however that stood out above all others. This day shook the whole surfing world, seeing waves this size in Newport is once in a lifetime event, and for the conditions to be so perfect for the whole swell everything couldn't have lined up more perfect. This day was September 24th, 2014. It was a Wednesday and the swell forecast leading up to this day seemed like a joke. Forecasts for the wedge Newport Beach was 30ft+, winds were supposed to be light all day, the angle of the swell for Newport Beach could not be more perfect. The evening before, my best friend and I had a quick session out at Newport point. Waves were about 10-12ft beautiful left handers in front of tower 17, the water was a deep dark green with a layer of foam covering the surface from the larger sets. The crowd was minimal, two surfers including myself and a small crowd of bodyboarders further down the line waiting to catch the corners. It was my birthday and being out with one of my local surfing idols Spencer Pirdy all by myself watching him pulling into these tubes so much deeper than what I thought was makeable blew my mind. He would drop in ten, twenty, thirty yards deeper then I would even dare, I thought for sure he was going to get sucked over the falls or have the wave close out on him every single time, but he always came shooting out over the backside of the wave with a big smile on his face. After a couple waves of watching him surf practically by himself when he paddled by me after a wave he asked "are you going to catch one? Or just sit and watch?". I told him I didn't think I could make it and he just said "well you will never know if you don't try". Right after that you could see the horizon once again welling up, a dark wall slowly forming and burrowing towards us, I remember I took a deep breath and just told myself "you better paddle hard or you're going to get f******". I lined myself up with the corner of the wave and dig deep with every stroke, I felt the wave lift my board up and I began to feel weightless as it started to suck up so much, it was from a hill to a small cliff in a matter of seconds , I did my best to grab rail and hook into my bottom turn, I made it to the bottom and rocketed down the line shaking the whole time as I rode past the bodyboarders barely holding on. Once I kicked out, I was hooked, adrenaline overtook me as it usually does when I surf larger waves now. I couldn't wipe the smile off my face, my lips would start to curl and cramp, and my whole body was shaking as I paddled back out to Spencer. I was so enthralled with making one of my first big waves out at Newport point. We ended up surfing til dark that night and got out when we didn't have much visibility left. I had finally surfed big Newport Point, I was on such a high that night driving back with my best friend Matt to his house. That was just the beginning though, once we got back to Matt's house, we checked the swell forecast for the next day. Just as it had been calling the past few weeks, the next day was going to be significantly larger, with better conditions. The forecast was still reading an easy 15ft for all of Newport, wedge forecast might as well have been 1000ft in my head at this point. We sat eating macaroni trying to figure out what our plan would be for the next day, we decided on waking up at the crack of dawn, before the sun was up, and to head straight to wedge. We headed to bed trying to make sure we would be ready and rested for the next day, but I couldn't sleep at all. After catching the waves, I did that evening and imaging It was going to be even larger the next day kept me up restless. I couldn't wait til 5am to wake up Matt so we could finally get going. After about ten minutes of shaking, jumping on him, and screaming at him to get up Matt and I made it to his little green Saturn that we called Catherine (our high school crush) and made our way to the beach. We first pulled up to 18th street at the Newport point and I didn't even think there were waves, I couldn't see a thing, there was this fog that was blocking the whole lineup and I thought we had all been gypped. Little did I know that fog, was not fog at all, it was mist from how large the surf was, I was being spews up into the air by the sets of 15ft plus Newport point. We made our way down to the wedge and what awaited for us could only be described as a medieval gauntlet. There were already thousands of people lined up on the burm line to watch the notorious wedge at her finest. Before we even got onto the sand, we could see a set large enough, it was taller than the lifeguard tower from our view. Game on, I instantly started shaking and breathing deeply as I realized how big it really was, and when I say shaking, I mean convulsing, because I knew I was going out there and I was $hit*** my pants. We made our way through the crowd with my board and just saw body's being bucked off of cliffs made up of water, 15ft, 18ft, 20ft + guys just going for it pulling into massive close outs and making the most impressive drops out of the air like it was nothing. We made our way towards the jetty where the normal local wedge crew usually is and we suited up. Matt decided that he was going to ride this one out on the sand but I was determined to at least paddle out so I could say I was out there. After preparing myself mentally as a 17 year old kid I saw a lull in the waves which means there were no sets to be seen. So myself, along with 5 other surfers or so, took off running down the sand towards the ice, the sand was so churned up it was like running through soup. To my surprise we made it out quite easily without having to go under one wave on the way out. I paddled way to the outside and to the right and set myself up in the best spot to just sit and watch. Over the next hour, I watched mountains, I'm not kidding, mountain sized sets roll through, I was watching guys drop into waves and the waves were four times as tall as they were! Some guys got sucked over in the lip, I thought to myself every time "oh yeah he's dead, yep him too, Awe I liked that guy that's a bummer"! It was so crazy to me that they all paddled back out, mostly smiling and livid wanting another!

Being inspired again I tried catching a couple of these mountains but being on a 5'9 shortboard in waves that large just was not working out for me, I opted to paddle to the inside and I caught the smallest wave possible and ran up the beach with the biggest smile, I didn't care if I didn't catch a set wave to impress the crowd, I was the one who got to go in the water while they sat on the beach. I finally found Matt in the crowd and we headed out straight to my dad's shop, I knew he had this 6'10 step up board for larger waves so we ran up to his shop and grabbed it. We called our other best friend Jonathan, and my little brother Dakota, let them know how big it was and proceeded to pick them up. Now that we were jam packed into Matt's Saturn with surfboards and bodysurfing fins and bodyboards we headed down to the upper jetties of Newport. We ended up at 44th street because it was the only parking we could find, and we ran out with our caravan of surfing equipment. Never before had I seen 44th liked we saw it that day. Once we got to the sand we saw heaven, no joke, just heavenly, beautiful, glassy, sunny waves, about 12-15ft A frame peaks, lefts and rights. With no one else out between 44th street and 48th. We all jumped in the water and just started pushing each other, daring each other, to go on waves and to go deeper every time. It ended up being the best session with my friends of my life. I had my brother and both my best friends from high school, I had just survived the wedge at 20ft+ waves. We had 44th street all to ourselves for almost four hours, with the most perfect surf you could ever want. After many, many waves, on different types of crafts, called it a day, we dragged ourselves back to the car and made a pit stop and headed back to Matt's, Matt and John stayed at his house and started playing grand theft auto, as my brother and I headed back home to fall asleep from a long morning of big surf. We made it home and all I did was walk inside the door, I walked toward my couch and just plopped right onto it, the boards still In the car and the wetsuits still soaked I passed out into a deep sleep, I was exhausted, I was so stoked, I didn't need anything else to finish that day out. But then I got a phone call from one of my best friends Jessica. She said she had heard how large the waves were and said she was going to surf Newport point. I told her I didn't think that was such a great idea as it was much larger than what she thought, but if you knew my friend Jessica you would know that she's determined. I asked her you're going to go even if I don't go with you aren't you, and she said yeah I'm going, no matter what. I told her well you're not giving me any choice I'm gonna have to go with you to make sure nothing happens. So, after already being wiped out and surfing the waves of my life Jessica picks me up along with my older brother who is going to shoot photos of us at the Newport point and we drove down in her little green car as well. Once we finally found parking because it was so packed now that the word got out how big it was, we ended up running down the beach looking at big windy waves. We had to run all the way to the pier because it was so big there's no way to paddle out at the point. Just the paddle out to the Newport point from the pier Took me about 45 minutes because the current was so strong, and I was already so exhausted. It ended up being another amazing session with only six other guys out including Jessica with once again big dark walls of water moving past us and eventually Cresting into a 15 foot plus wave. After being out in the water for about two hours I remember I only caught about five or six waves and I know Jessica got at least two. I caught a left that I thought I was going to eat crap on. I sunk my weight into my legs and got as low as I could so I made the drop. I made the drop, I came around a big section it was just a big wall, my legs were shaking I could barely see the wave as well as it was already dark at this point after I gave it my best effort the web finally took off

45

without me so I laid down on my stomach and ride that wave in to find my brother on the beach. After being on the beach for about 20 minutes we finally saw the largest side of the day come through and Jessica was the only one left out in the water after she made it over the first one two and then three waves we just remember watching the fourth wave probably around 18 foot landed right on her head after that we couldn't find her. We running up and down the beach looking for her and it took about another 15 to 30 minutes until we finally saw her running up the beach. Once that weight broke on her head she got sucked all

the way down the beach past the pier and was able to finally paddling on the other side of the pier near Blackies. Freaking all of us out on the beach trying to find her she ran up with a big smile on her face and said that was the scariest and most amazing thing she had done. This was the swelling this was the exact day that me and all my friends started to push each other in bigger waves and this is when we realize that we were going to be hooked for a very long time chasing waves like this for the rest of our lives. This by far was one of the most amazing days in my life surfing I got to surf with all the most important people in my life, I got to push myself just getting the guts to even paddle out at the wedge, and we got to push each other me and my friends to take off on waves that we usually wouldn't go on the conditions were so beautiful all day with the sun being out all day long in the winter only coming up the last couple hours of sunlight. This was my best day in surfing

-RIVER MUNGALL
Local Surfer, Massage Therapist, Holistic Health Practitioner

I think when you ask about my Best Day, it certainly wasn't on the football field. I played football for 12 years, and I had broken my Achilles tendon and I was basically lost. I was divorced and I was going out on a trip when an airline stewardess told me about a man who taught the bible on TV, his name was Apostle Fred Price. I walked away from her, but she came back and asked me for my phone number, so I gave it to her. Sunday morning, my phone rang, and a man named Ken Ludwig called saying, "My wife told me to call you to watch the man on TV who teaches the bible, Fred Price." I said, "I don't know a Ken Ludwig." But he told me that his wife told him to call me. Ken Ludwig told me to turn on channel 11 at 8:30 to listen to the man speak on the bible. It was an almighty great day for me, because I called my son and we both listened.

One Saturday night, soon after, my son asked me to take him to church, and I told him that I didn't want to go to church. My son said, "But dad, I have never been to Church." Of course, that put a pain in my heart, so I said we will go one day, and so we went. We heard the gospel of Jesus Christ, how he died on a cross to forgive us for our sins and gave us our right to become a member of the family of God by asking him into our hearts. It changed my life, and it's never been the same. It helps me to become a better person every day because he said, "He'll never leave us nor forsake us." (John 3:16)

-ROSEY GRIER
Defensive Tackle, NY Giants, LA Rams 2X Pro Bowler, 3X All Pro

The best time of my life in Sports. The Thrilla in Manila, Ali-Frazier III in Manila, October 1, 1975. TKO 14.

Without question the singular, most electrifying moment came as Round 14 was about to begin. Round 13 had seen Ali give Frazier an inhuman pounding, Frazier, half blind, his face a mass of lumps, bumps, cuts and bruises managed to stay upright. How I don't know. He fell into his corner, I saw a brief argument as his wise, old corner man signaled "No More". Joe could not get up, but his legs wouldn't carry him. My best moment: THAT ONE.

-FERDIE PACHECO

Doctor and cornerman for Muhammad Ali

My Best Days were The Joe Frazier fights!

-MUHAMMAD ALI

Boxer, 3X WBC heavyweight champion, 6X Ring Magazine Fighter of the Year,3X WBA heavyweight champion, 2X Golden Glove Champion, 1960 Olympic Gold Medalist, Sports Illustrated Sportsman of the Century

My Best Days were every one of the Ali fights- but the first one when I won and became of Heavy Weight Champion of the World was the absolute best.

-JOE FRAISER

Professional Boxer, Heavy Weight Champion 1970-1973, Gold Medalist 1964 Tokyo, 32 wins, 27 by KO, 4 losses, 1 draw

My Best Day is every day I'm able to wake up and play the game I love--BASKETBALL!

-TAMIKA CATCHINGS

WNBA Player; Indiana Fever, 2011 WNBA MVP, 10X All-Star, 5X Defensive Player of the Year

My Best Day was July 2, 1989--the day I married my wife
Janet.

-MIKE PATRICK
*ESPN sportscaster, Former Play-by-Play
announcer Sunday Night Football*

My Best Day is today as our creator, God-has blessed us all
with the opportunity to live each day
at our own choice. I am blessed to be alive today and only
hope someone else's life is made better by
something I might do today.

-KEN HATFIELD

Head Football Coach, Air Force, University of Arkansas, Clemson & Rice,
3 SWC Championships, 1 ACC Championship

My Best Day was my final game before retirement. It was great to score 60 points, but it was the support that meant so much. Watching the video; and to see how far I have come after 20 years. I had received so many well-wishes and good-byes all season, but to have my final game on the home court, with my wife, kids, family and friends all there...it was the best.

-KOBE BRYANT

LA Lakers, 5X National Champion, 2X MVP NBA Finals,
14 X NBA All-Star, 4X All-Star MVP,
2008 & 2012 Gold Medal Champion- Basketball

Ironically my Best Day in football did not occur in high school, college or for that matter in the National Football League. It occurred 65 years ago on a grassy field in my hometown of Warren, Ohio. The setting was Packard Park, an iconic venue, which hosted numerous sporting contests. This event was the city of Warren's grade school championship football game. I was a member of First Street Elementary School's touch football team. We were paired against Laird Avenue Elementary School for the title. I recall the game being a tight struggle late in the fourth quarter. The score was tied 12 all with the clock winding down to zero. The position I played was called end in those days. Today it is referred to as wide receiver. As time was running out First Street possessed the football with a final opportunity to win. Our quarterback Willie Jones had a phenomenal ability to throw the long ball. He called for a deep post pattern in our huddle. When the ball was snapped, I immediately got behind Laird Avenue School's secondary in the middle of the field. As I looked back, I saw a sphere launched and headed on a trajectory in perfect proximity to where I was running. All I had to do was watch the ball arrive in my hands. I did exactly so! I then ran as fast as I could to the end zone untouched. The clock ran out and my alma mater, First Street Elementary School was city champions. It was a meaningful experience for me. My very first, as a member of a championship team. After our prestigious victory the principal at First Street School feted our team with a special recognition luncheon. The food fair was hot dogs and coke. It was great!!

There is an old axiom that is appropriate to paraphrase here, "
first experiences are the most memorable one's".   First Street
School's championship win was the first I experienced.
Additionally; our team was so efficient that we finished our
season not only as city champions, but we were also untied as
well as undefeated. Little did I know at the time that years later
I would again play for a historical National Football League
championship team (Miami Dolphins) that was and still is to
this day, the only untied and undefeated team in the annals of
the NFL. I have immense pride in being a member of the
undefeated 1972 Miami Dolphins; however, First Street
School's undefeated team was equally meaningful because it
was the "FIRST" major team accomplishment I experienced.

-PAUL WARFIELD
Pro Football Hall of Fame Wide Receiver, Cleveland Browns,
Miami Dolphins, 2X Super Bowl Championship; 8X Pro Bowler,

My Best Memory in college was being part of the Purdue's first Rose Bowl team. We won, beating USC 14-13.

My Best Memory in the Pros was playing in three consecutive Super Bowl games with the Miami Dolphins, the last two of which we won, culminating in the '72 team's perfect season record of 17-0.

My Best Memory in my 30-year broadcasting career was working with Keith Jackson, including 10 Rose Bowls- the highlight of which was covering the game when my son Brian with Michigan won the National Championship.

-BOB GRIESE

NFL Quarterback, Miami Dolphins, 2X Super Bowl Champion, 6X Pro Bowl, NFL MVP 1971, Hall of Fame

Thank you for including me—The Best Day of my life was the birth of my daughters; both of them, followed by beating the Boston Celtics on the parquet floor in 1985.

GARY VITTI

LA Lakers, Head Athletic Trainer.

My very Best Day was a fall day in 1974 my freshman year in college. It was the day I was led to the realization that Jesus was God and he gave His life a payment for my many shortcomings. That God loved me so much that he suffered so that I might be holy in His eyes. He uses me on a regular basis since then and my next best day included any day that he does. Lots of awards and achievements, but none stack up to God's Love and my joy as a result. Hopefully He has made His love evident to you as well.

You can do all things in Christ's Strength. 4:13

DOUG SMITH

NFL Center, Guard; Los Angeles Rams, 6X Pro Bowl

I like all of the people that you have written I would have to say that May 7, 2017 was my wife's Best Day on a beautiful spring day, we were driving back from my grandson's graduation from grad school at University of Kentucky just outside White Sulfur Springs in West Virginia on Route 64 when tractor-trailer passed us on a two-lane stretch going east, he lost sight of us evidently because he tried to get over in my lane we were caught up under the truck and I could not disengage the truck and the driver realized what had he had done and overcorrected and turned over. We all bailed out down the median siding sideways we went down into the median and passed out pointed West in the westbound lane my side was crushed and only because the roof did not totally cave in. I was spared, my wife side was not affected and good Samaritan pulled me out of the collapsed side through the door on my wife's side needless to say many things could have happened could've been crushed we had we not slid sideways rather than entering the median abruptly the car could've been flipped down a steep embankment on the west side of westbound car could attest the car was totaled of course but we did not have a scratch, that was our Best Day.

-KEN WILLARD
Fullback; San Francisco 49ers, St. Louis Cardinals

My best day was in September 1975 when I won my 20th game in San Diego against the Dodgers.
I was the first Padre to ever win twenty games.

-RANDY JONES

MLB San Diego Padres;
NL Cy Young Winner, 2X All-Star

I have a couple of days I could consider my Best Days, but I would have to go with the days my nephews were born. Ages five and three (in 2003) they are my world and I couldn't imagine having my good days if they weren't around.

-JENNIFER BUTLER
WNBA Basketball Center, Cleveland Rockies

My Best Day in football was with the Rams, the 1985 season. It was the best, I was voted All-Pro 1st team and I played in the Pro Bowl game.

-RON BROWN

NFL Wide Receiver, LA Rams,
Oakland Raiders, 1985 Pro Bowl.

Sunday, August 11, 1974

I decided to write about "one" of my very Best Days in golf!
There certainly have been more than one, but a day in 1974 was
very special.

The very first Colgate European Open was hosted at
Sunningdale Golf Club outside London in August of '74. For
starters, I was a very good player at the time, but not the best.
My great fortune was that the best and most renowned caddy
there ask to work for me, Mr. Ron Mullins, or "Mull" as
everyone knew him. 65 years old and at the club since he was
13 made him very knowledgeable. He was a big part of my
love affair with Sunningdale that endures to this day.

I had never been very sentimental about golf or courses until my
experience there. For the first time I had a real appreciation for
where the game started and history!

As for my history that week, it went like this. It was my 2nd or
3rd event with a new graphite (carbonite) driver. Mull
convinced me to play the small ball and he grabbed my hand
firmly when I reached for my 5 iron from heather, handed me a
sand wedge and nodded yes.

Sunningdale is a parkland/heathland course with some links characteristics. No irrigation systems at that time, so completely natural. I liked it right away. Drove the ball very well and Mull read the putts. Long story short, we won. It felt special because it was there, certainly equaling the happiness of winning.

I cannot prove it, but I believe I may have been the first player to win with a graphite shaft and the last American player to win with the small ball.

Mull remained my friend and my husband, Yippy's friend, until the end of his life. Lots of life lessons and help come from unexpected people!

Sunningdale did a picture and feature on me in their 100-year anniversary book. So grateful to have experienced the place and having been able to visit as time has gone on.

-JUDY RANKIN
Professional Golfer, LPGA Tour Winner
& Player of the Year 1976 & 1977, 26 Career wins

My Best Day had to be playing in the Masters in 1985 with my uncle Bob Goalby and brother Jay Haas.
As I look back, being in the prestigious Master's with the professionals from the same family, it is something I'll always cherish.

-JERRY HAAS

Men's Head Golf Coach, Wake Forest University;
Professional Golfer

My Best Day was in June of 1975, I went 5-6 with three hits, one triple, one single and ten RBIs. The only out I made was a line drive out to second. We won 15-1!

-FRED LYNN

MLB Baseball Center Fielder; Boston Red Sox,
California Angels, Baltimore Orioles, San Diego Padres;
9X All-Star, AL Rookie or the Year & MVP 1975, 4X Golden Glove

One of my Best Days was being drafted into the NFL
by the Detroit Lions. I must admit I have had too many
Best Days to limit it to 1.

-LOMAS BROWN
Detroit Lions, NY Giants, Offensive Tackle

Hitting a home run in the 1943 All Star Game, we won 5-3 in Philadelphia.

-BOBBY DOERR

MLB 2nd Baseman, Boston Red Sox, 9X All-Star,
1943 World Series Champion, Baseball Hall of Fame

I would have to say my Best Day was the birth of my little girl (Kelsey Ann) on 8/28/2000. I am about to have my second child on 5/28/2003 and I know that will be another Best Day.

-KRISTY CURRY
Purdue Women's Basketball Coach

My Best Day in racing was last summer at Del Mar when Famous Digger won the Grade One Del Mar Oaks. It was so special because I had claimed Famous Digger earlier in the year from Richard Mandella for $40,000.00. I had been watching her in the mornings and she worked great, but in the afternoon when she would go to race, she would be a complete nut in the paddock and on the track.

-BARRY ABRAMS
Professional Horse Trainer, 600+ career wins

Having been at USC during the early 2000's when we were dominating, it is pretty hard to say what my BEST Day is. I can say, my first day on campus was my best day, finally being able to say I was a legit Trojan. I was a Spring Enrollee due to my SAT scores. I had not taken the test serious because I was informed by someone who was not a coach that I did not need to pass, because I would be accepted anyways. Well, I soon found out that the story I was told was just that, A Story. So, I found myself sitting at home watching USC play during that 2002 season and not playing with them. Once I found out I was not eligible to play, I retook the test and passed. Unfortunately, I was still forced to sit out for the season and had to enroll into school that Spring of 2003. So finally, being on campus could be my best day.

I can even discuss the first game I played in against Auburn in 2003. As we were on our way to the game on the team bus, our bus actually went into a ditch to avoid a crash. Many would assume this to be a scary moment, but not, not for us Trojans. Instead of everyone being nervous, we actually all started rocking the bus while we were in the ditch. This occurrence actually got us fired up even more for the game... Or how about being a True Freshmen starting in his first game against Auburn who had a stacked team full of players who would later turn Professional soon after. On the opening drive for Auburn, our treacherous defense got after the quarterback Jason Campbell forcing him to roll out. As he threw the ball, Kevin Arbet actually got a hand on it preventing it from being a catch for Auburn and it eventually turning into an interception. This would be My First Game as a Trojan, My First Start as a Trojans, and now My First Interception as a Trojan.

I can go on the say that another Best Day could be when we played Michigan in the Rose Bowl. Which lead to us being the Co-Champions this year to our outstanding play during the course of the season.

The 2004 season was completely dominated by our team. No one we faced during this season stood a chance against us, which was amazing. The beauty about this is the fact that we knew we were great, but we still went out there to practice and into each game knowing we had to give our best. Often times, when people are aware of how great they are, they tend to slack a bit and put themselves in situations they could have avoided had they prepared properly. Preparing properly was something we did each week.

The 2005 was a great season for us as well, even with the loss against Texas... A great Day can be with me scoring the First Touchdown of the season on an interception against Hawaii. The entire week was crazy for me. I had food poison as we flew to Hawaii and then during the entire week we spent there preparing for the game, but as we got closer to game time, I was able to recover completely and I had a pretty good game in addition to my pick 6 early in the game.

Another great day could be against Notre Dame. As you are aware, this is a huge rivalry game for us, depending on the season, this game can mean more than the game against that other school down the road from USC. LOL. However, we went into this game ready to fight as always, and so did they. This game went to the wire. I can remember a big play I had that played a big role in our victory. We were in cover 3 and I was covering my flats area and I see Brady Quinn throw a dart to Anthony Fasano, so I flipped my hips and ran. As I was getting closer, I was observing him and realized that I had a great chance of doing something BIG. As I got to him, I punched the ball out and pulled him down, the ball flew nearly 10 yards away and Keith Rivers scooped the ball up, giving us the chance to prevent a score and potentially march down the field and score. As I stated earlier, this game went to the wire. The final drive of the game was a course of miracles. Dwayne Jarrett caught a deep ball on 4th down I believe as he was dealing with issues from his eye contacts. Later in the drive, Matt Leinart rolled out and dove for the endzone and the ball was knocked out of his hands flying into the air, but gratefully for us, it went out of bounds. The entire stadium cleared the stands as they assumed the game was over and rushed the field. What a huge mistake. They all were forced to get off the field as a few seconds were placed back on the clock and the following play Matt Leinart ran a sneak and got us the victory.

The Fresno State game is another game that went down to the wire. Another all out battle against another great team. This game, Reggie Bush had over 500 yards himself (what an amazing game he had). I had two interceptions myself to end the game. One which was for a touchdown but later called back on a felonious penalty, the referees certainly made a bad call on this play here. The second interception came later in the game with Fresno State going for a Touchdown to seal the deal. It was obvious that the Quarterback felt his receiver was much better than the defenders in this play or he was simply hoping for a miracle. Either way, he was wrong on this play or his miracle just didn't come in time. I intercepted the pass in the end zone where I clearly knew I needed to kneel down, but I ran it out and eventually gained 40 yards to seal the deal for another Trojan victory. This game would also be the last game I would play in the Coliseum (What a glorious way to go out).

I provide these examples for you to give you an idea of what comes to mind when I think of My Best Day. However, none of these will be considered my best day. My Best Day as a Trojan fell in May of 2013. I returned back to school in August of 2012 to finish up my last year of school to earn my degree. In May 2013, I was officially able to say I was a certified USC Alumni. I needed 34 units to earn my degree and I finally did it. I was finally a True USC Alumni. This was My Best Day as a USC Trojan by far. I was never the best student nor was I the greatest kid to have in your class growing up. I have been told by many growing up that I would not amount to anything. However, May of 2013, I was able to say I had graduated from one of the most prestigious institutions in the world. This would lead to the inspiration to continue to be great and further my knowledge. In May 2016, I later earned my Master's Degree from USC as well.

-DARNELL BING, M. Ed

USC Football Strong Safety; Line Backer, Oakland Raiders, SF 49ers, NY Jets, Detroit Lions

The day my sons were born is my Best Day.

-MIKE BROWN
Head NBA Coach, Cleveland Cavaliers & LA Lakers,
Assistant NBA Coach, Golden State Warriors, 2017 NBA Champions

The best day of my basketball life was the first day I ran out on the floor wearing a St. Louis Hawk uniform with Bob Pettit on one side, Cliff Hagan on the other and Lenny Wilkens leading me to my first NBA game.

-GENE TORMOHLEN

Head Scout, Los Angeles Lakers, NBA Power Forward, Washington Nationals, St. Louis/ Atlanta Hawks

Greatest day: 1978 Yankees World Series victory and the 1981 World Series vs the Yankees on as a Dodger. It was when I pinch hit the go-ahead home run to win the game off Ron Guidry.
Billy Martin was the best manager; Tom Lasorda more fun and the best to play for.

-JAY JOHNSTONE

MLB Outfielder, Anaheim Angels, Chicago White Sox, New York Yankees, Los Angeles Dodgers, 2X World Series Champ

Central Michigan University Department of Athletics, my Alma Mater, named the academic center in my honor. The Dick Enberg Academic Center was dedicated on October 12, 2007. It was good to give back to a school that accepted a total nobody and allowed me to be somebody.

-DICK ENBERG

Sportscaster, 13 Sports Casting Emmys; Ranked top 50 sportscaster of all time, Pete Rozelle Award from the NFL Hall of Fame

My "Best Day" was on my 31st birthday!

Greg, my son, our first child, was born healthy.

-BARRY SWITZER

Head Coach, University of Oklahoma, NFL Dallas Cowboys,
Winner, Super Bowl XXX

My Best Day? Today!

Every day is a special day at this stage of life. But, the one day I cherish in my coaching career was June 9th, 1985 at the Boston Garden. Game 6, the Lakers beat the Celtics 111-110 on the parquet floor.

-BILL BERTKA

Former NBA executive New Orleans Jazz, Assistant Coach, LA Lakers, 6X NBA Championship - Lakers

Of all my play-by-play moments, the one that remains the most vivid is Minnesota's victory over Michigan at Michigan Stadium in 1986. Michigan was a top-heavy favorite but had to struggle to tie the Gophers at 21-21.

Then in the last minute of play, quarterback Rickey Foggie ran a zigzag course from Minnesota territory deep enough into Michigan territory to put the ball within field goal range. The run seemed almost slow motion to me as I watched it get closer to that field goal distance and then within it.

Two plays later Chip Lohmiller kicked a field goal for a 24-21 Gopher upset, the clock read zero, and over 100,000 Michigan fans sat there in stunned silence.

The silence is what I remember; most of all-the most wonderful non-sound I have ever heard in a Gopher game.

-RAY CHRISTIANSEN
Announcer, University of Minnesota

"My Best Day" originates in Iowa City, Iowa in 1971-1972. My father, Jack, was taking my brother John (10) and me to school in freezing, cold, Iowa for his like and wintery weather. Apparently, our enthusiasm level was not high enough for his liking and one morning he proclaimed "attack this day with enthusiasm unknown to mankind. And" he added, "don't take any wooden nickels. (Don't get rolled over) This mantra was repeated for months.

Both John and I have come to the understanding that TODAY is our "Best Day."

I strive to make today better than yesterday and tomorrow better than today.

-JIM HARBAUGH
NFL Quarterback, Chicago Bears, Indianapolis Colts, San Diego Chargers, 1995 Pro Bowl; Head Football Coach, SF 49ers, NFL Champions 2011; Head Football Coach, Stanford University, University of Michigan

Every day I have participated in a sport, as a player, coach or a parent has been a best day. I have made lifelong friends, learned valuable lessons, dealt with adversity and experienced success. I now have the joy of watching my own two children enjoy this same journey, I think these experiences will help them become the best people they can be.

-STEVE CONTI

Head Volleyball Coach, Corona Del Mar High School, Boys CIF Champions 1998, 2000,2005,2007,2011 & 2017, 2016 Coach of the Year, Girls 1997 CIF Champions

My best UCLA day was the day before the NCAA Championship finals in 2011, when for the first time I actually deeply felt the intellectual knowledge, that it was all about the journey and the relationships made along the way...not about the title itself,

-MICHEAL SEALY

UCLA Head Women's Volleyball Coach, 2011 National Champions, As player, UCLA, 1993 National Champion

My best day was the day my first child, a boy named Luke, was born on March 16, 1985. My wife and I had suffered through several miscarriages and to have a healthy baby made it the greatest day of my life.

-MIKE BELLOTTI

Head Football Coach, Chico State, University of Oregon, 2014 College Football Hall of Fame

My life to this point has been a continuation of my best day as a Trojan. I can remember like it was yesterday, the whole recruiting process. The trip to Notre Dame with Marty Patton, meeting Sam Cunningham at the CIF Track and Field Championships, talking with impressive Dick Vermiel at Stanford and the imposing Tommy Prothro at UCLA. All these events were crammed into the process of choosing which University I would go to, free of charge, to play a sport I had come to love, get an education and meet the woman I would marry. On campus, it was like daily portraying a part in a feature length movie. Like the ones I had watched about the Gipper or Red Grange or Jim Thorpe. The cast of characters in this epic was unique and well defined. There was Rod Humenuik, Willie Brown, Craig Fertig, Dave Levy, and of course; John McKay. And these were just the coaches. The players were equally fascinating and talented. But it was the atmosphere of USC... that was it!!! The mere fact of being there in the hallowed halls where all the prior greats had walked, studied, bled, lost and won. It was the whole thing. The dorms, the old locker room and training facility and the wood trimmed coaches offices. It was all part of the setting of this magical experience we were having being Trojans.

One of the seemingly minor items that had an impact on me was the bell. It tolled regularly, calling out the hour, quarter hour and half hour, I believe. It also served as a constant reminder to me that we were in reality and not in some dream state. The same bell was heard by everyone on campus and even some in the neighborhood.

It communicated in its own way the importance of what our mission was at USC. Play the highest quality and level of football the way it was meant to be played and get an education. The education part was something that was a family necessity. My parents stressed it and it was almost automatic that we; all nine of us children of Robert and Julia McNeill, would get a college education. These items were at the forefront of my mind.

But the best day of many best days as a Trojan was this particular day, in my second year at USC. We were staying in one of the dorms at USC as we were in the throes of fall training camp. During our off time some of the new incoming girls had come over to our dorm to meet some of the players. There was one girl in particular who caught my eye. Her name was Pamela. It would take some time before we would get to the point of becoming husband and wife and it was all my fault. It wasn't until the 32nd year of our marriage the full impact of the incredibly excellent occurrence meeting my wife.

The event that caused that awakening was me getting tonsil cancer. I elected to have surgery to remedy the cancer issue. The day I checked into the hospital at USC Medical Center at 5:00am I ran into a former teammate who was also having a minor procedure. I always look for confirmations in life that to me act as markers or signposts that let me know I am on the right track. Some would call them coincidences, but I saw them as much more meaningful.

My surgery that day lasted for 10 hours and the first thing I remember when I awoke was seeing my wife smiling at me. She has the most wonderful smile. When I saw that smile, I knew I was going to be ok. But it was what happened during the 12 days I stayed in the hospital recovering that helped me to fully understand how special that day was when I met Pamela. I had undergone some very delicate and serious surgery by the excellent USC team. My recovery involved some pretty substantial pain meds that resulted in me having some very strange and frightening dreams. I would wake every night around 3:00am terrified and my wife would be right there. She stayed by my side for 12 days, sleeping in a small chair next to my bed. I don't think I would have made it through that ordeal if she had not been there. I really owe her my life. That makes the day I met her indeed My Best Day as a Trojan!

-ROD MCNEILL
USC Running Back, NFL New Orleans Saints, Tampa Bay Buccaneers

I feel my best day was back in 1976. At the beginning of the year, my life agent Colin Wicks and I decided to try to become the first jockey to win 500 races in a single season. Bill Shoemaker held the record with 486 wins.

It was a long year; but by the end we had 515 wins. Our goal was 500 and it was the most memorable.
The horses' name was Charlie Be, the track was Laurel Race Track in Maryland. That was my biggest day and biggest thrill.

-SANDY HAWLEY
Hall of Fame Horse Jockey

Am honored and humbled by your request for "My Best Day."
At 68 years old now, with four children and seven
grandchildren, you can imagine all the good days God provides
for us. However, as a former athlete, I wanted to share a story
that is about a particular day…January 9, 1977.

But first, let me tell you about my dad, Richard E. Bankston,
born in 1907. He was an athlete himself, and he and my mother
raised three boys, all of us playing as many sports as we
could… football, basketball, track and baseball. But all three
boys excelled in football. My two older brothers both played
college football, but did not go any further, as I did.

In 1965, my freshman year at Tulane, my dad passed away
without seeing me play a single college game. He himself
played at Tulane, and as the record books will reveal, Tulane's
1931 Green Wave Team went 11-0, and then proceeded to play
in the Rose Bowl against USC on January 1, 1932. It was a sad
day, as Tulane lost 21-12 to USC. I had chosen Tulane because
my dad had wanted one of his three boys to play at his alma
mater. Although recruited by many schools out of high school, I
chose Tulane, a private school in New Orleans, Louisiana. I
loved my dad, I respected him, and I wanted to follow in his
footsteps as a Tulane Greenie.

Little did I know that in 1969, I would be drafted by the Steelers in the second round, and subsequently play 4 years for them under the guidance of Chuck Noll. With a clear view of me from heaven, I'm sure my dad enjoyed seeing his son be part of a World Championship team on a field where he had played many years prior to my appearance on the same turf. In my heart, this game was for him. As the Raider Nation cheered for us as victors, I'm sure that my dad enjoyed the applause for the Raiders that had eluded his great Tulane team, but was happy for me to be part of a Championship Team, erasing the sad memory of their loss in Pasadena and replaced by our victory. On the field, this was my "best day" and hopefully, it was a great day for my dad as well. I am sure that he had a great seat.

-WARREN BANKSTON

NFL Player, Pittsburg Steelers, Oakland Raiders, Super Bowl XI Champion, University of Tulane Riptides

In the athletic world, "My Best Day" occurred when I received a call from the Naismith Memorial Basketball Hall of Fame.

That I would be enshrined with the class of 1997. This enshrinement validated my career as a player for 12 years in the National Basketball Association.

-BAILEY HOWELL

NBA Small Forward, Detroit Pistons, Boston Celtics, Philadelphia 76ers, 2X NBA Championship, 6X All-Star, NBA Hall of Fame-

1) Making the 1972 Olympic Team

2) To finally win a championship at the highest level of play. That was the greatest and to go to the 3 finals with two different teams; that was a great accomplishment!

-TOM HENDERSON

NBA Shooting Guard, Atlanta Hawks, Washington Bullets, Houston Rockets. 1978 NBA Champion

Qualifying for the 1996 Olympic Games at 39 years old was my best day. I had played for 20 years and helped the sport grow from an amateur Southern California weekend party to a nationwide professional sport to an international professional sport to the Olympic Games. Each step along the way fed the next until 1996 when I could say that I played a major role in getting the sport to the Olympic Games and beyond. I can look back and say I wasn't just a great player but built something that the whole world can enjoy.

Having children with my wife was, and is, pretty spectacular!

-SINJIN SMITH

Pro Beach Volleyball Player, US Champion, 2 World Championships,
UCLA 1979 National Champions

My Best Day of
surfing took place in 2009 in Indonesia. It was a surf spot
known as G-Land on the island of Java. The waves were
flawless perfection, and just my best friend Justin McBride and
I were out alone trading off the best waves we had ever surfed.
The waves were about 6-10 feel face speedies. We were getting
at least 10-15
Second tube rides by ourselves, it was a real dream! The ocean
temperature was 80 degrees and aqua colored that you could see
all the fish and reef below. We surfed for 8 hours, and a full
moon which makes the waves bigger and better. We were there
with our friends Darreyl Goodram and Dennis DeWitt, who
were convinced they had malaria. They stayed inside and slept
while Justin and I got every type of backside barrel you could
imagine. We will remember that day our whole lives, we were
living the dream!

My other best day was when I won my 1st ASP WAQ event in
Mexico, in San Miguel, Ensenada in 2001. I was amazed, and it
felt so insane to stand on the podium and have won. I won
money and qualifying points. The other finalists were Pat
Gudauskis, Benji Severson and Heremy Sherwin. I was 21 years
old and amazed. We partied hard after that and will never forget
that feeling; I will be in the history books forever. Super stoked.

-MATT KING
Professional Surfer

My Best Sports Day, coming from a pure amateur athlete's perspective, was when I ended up on stage at the Shrine Auditorium in downtown Los Angles,…standing right next to Ray Charles and his weathered piano, while he performed his classic rendition of "America the Beautiful" to a packed house and TV audience.

A close second would have to be kissing Nancy Reagan on the cheek at the Presidential Breakfast the morning following the closing ceremonies of the 1984 Los Angeles Olympic Games.

-TIM SHAW
Water Polo/ Swimmer; Silver Medal winner,
1976 Olympics -swimming & Silver Medal winner, 1984
Olympics- Water Polo

I don't have one best day game to give, given my coaching record and talk of success. They are all my best days because of tremendous parents and now due to a great wife and four children, I have been blessed. I am thankful for a great life.

-BILL RAFTERY

Head Basketball Coach, Farileigh-Dickenson-Madison, Seton Hall
1976-77 National Champions, Basketball Announcer

I have had a great many best days, I don't know what "the Best Day" is? I will list what are memorable "great, good, fulfilling days. I do hope the Best Day is yet to come.

1) The day I married my wife. 57 years ago (in 2008)
2) The opening ceremony of the 48 Olympic Games in 1948
3) The day of the birth of each of our children- we have four: 2 boys & 2 girls.
4) Every day when I can wakeup and appreciated reasonably good health, and the company of a few good friends.

-BOB KENARD
AAU Center, Phillips 66ers, 3X AAU Champion;
Olympic Gold Medalist Basketball, London 1948 & Helsinki 1952

I have been lucky in that I have had so many best days--from the first win at Northwestern University to the Super Bowl win with San Francisco, to being named head coach at Stanford and later with the Vikings. They are all moments I will never forget.

-DENNIS GREEN

NFL Head Football Coach, Minnesota Vikings, Arizona Cardinals

It is very easy for me to tell you that the best day that I had was the day that I married my lovely wife, Mary Jane.

-ROLAND V. MASSIMINO

Head Basketball Coach, Villa Nova and Cleveland State,
NCAA Division I Champions 1985-Villa Nova, College Hall of Fame

I have had many Best Days. I believe that if we keep a positive attitude, we can strive to make every day a good day.

-ORLANDO "TUBBY" SMITH

Head Basketball Coach, University of Kentucky, University of Minnesota, Texas Tech

1963 - Marrying Diane.

1967 - First Major League game with Detroit.

1985 - Broadcasting Pete Roses' 4,291st hit.

1990s - The wedding days of our daughters and birth of four grandchildren.

-DAVE CAMPBELL

ESPN Sportscaster; MLB Player, Detroit Tigers, St Louis Cardinals, Houston Astros

My Best Days were the days my kids were born. The Saturday night I hosted my first Sports Center was also pretty exciting. I'd worked on ESPN2 for several months and wanted the chance to prove I could do the "big show." I'd set the goal of doing *Sports Center* as a teenager. Accomplishing that was a big kick.

-RECE DAVIS

ESPN Sportscaster

The Best Day of my life would be my wedding day. Pamela Moore Shyatt is my best friend and has been for 25 years. We have three beautiful sons that came from our union and whatever may or may not happen in our lifetime…that day will always be the most precious, most memorable, the Best Day of my life.

-LARRY SHYATT

Head Basketball Coach, Clemson University, Wyoming,
WAC Coach of the Year 1998

My Best Days have always been those where I am able to put a smile on a face that was in desperate need of one. But lately, I have found it to be my very best day when I hear the words, "I love you, Grandpa!"

-JOE HARPER

President, Del Mar Thoroughbred Club

It's hard to pick one Best Day when you go to a school like USC, however, one of my best days at SC was winning my first pairs AVCA beach championship.

I loved being part of an emerging NCAA sport as it gained momentum throughout the nation. Bringing the championship to USC meant being able to give back to a school that has given so much to me. Being a part of such an amazing program has given me skills that will last throughout my lifetime. I am so grateful for my experiences on and off the court. Fight on!

-KIRBY BURNHAM

USC Indoor and Sand Volleyball, AVCA 2014 Champion, 2014 All-American

The Best Day of my life was when my daughter, Siobhan was born. It felt like Christmas morning. Actually, it <u>was</u> Christmas morning, December 25th, 2004.

-REBECCA LOBO

WNBA Center, NY Liberty, Houston Comets, Connecticut Sun, 1989 WNBA All-Star, Basketball Hall of Fame, Gold Medalist, Atlanta 1996.

I can't narrow down to one "Best Day in Basketball." However, I do have 2 days that stick in my mind. In 1998 and 2008 we won the State Championship at Arco Arena in Sacramento. There was so much joy and happiness amongst the team, the staff and our fans. The feeling of accomplishment was fantastic, I was so happy and proud of my team. To experience this once is great, to have this feeling again was just phenomenal. These two experiences were "my best days in basketball."

-JERRY DEBUSK

Head Basketball Coach, Newport Harbor High, Santa Margarita High School. 1998 & 2008 State Champions

The day my girls filled the medal stand, all 45 of them, to receive the Southwest Regional Championship Women's Points trophy. As fate may have it that year, I was alone coaching these girls in all levels and disciplines of rowing. But the one thing we had going for us is we never lost sight of being a team and that day there was not a dry eye on that podium.

-CHRISTY SHAVER

Head Coach, Director of Junior Rowing, Newport Aquatic Center; Singles Rower

My Best Day would have to be winning my first Kentucky Derby on Winning Colors; I'd have to say what Eddie Arcaro said (in the first *My Best Day* book), "I'd never thought I'd ride in a Kentucky Derby, let alone win three!"

-GARY STEVENS

Hall of Fame Horse Jockey, Eclipse Outstanding
Jockey 1998, Actor; Sea Biscuit

I have had a great many Best Days. I don't know what "The Best Day' is so I will list what are memorable great, god, fulfilling days. I do hope the Best Day is yet to come.

1)   The day married my wife 57 years ago
2)   The opening ceremony of the 48 Olympic Games in London 1948.
3)   The day of the birth of each of our children. We have four, 2 boys & 2 girls
4)   Every day when I can wake up and appreciate reasonably good health and the company of a few old friends.

-BOB KURTLAND

NBA Center, Philadelphia 76ers, 2X NCAA Champion, Sporting News Player of the year, NBA Basketball Hall of Fame, College Basketball Hall of Fame, Olympic Gold Medalist, 1948-London & 1952 Helsinki

I have to say my Best Day was in June of 1981 at the Steve Prefontaine track and field meet in Eugene, Oregon where I was to race the best in the world in the 800 meters. I only finished fourth behind Olympian Randy Wilson and Kenyan Mike Boyt, but this day gave birth to a new man and eventually a sub 3:47 mile. On this day--I became the runner that I dreamed. I became the runner that now instills hard work and dedication as pillars into the minds of kids and my beloved four children, Bucko, Trevor, Christina and Danielle.

-BRIAN THERIOT
Track Team Captain, UCLA, world-class runner

I will admit that some days are better than others and winning the World Series would be a great day to add to my list! But as long as I have my family, my friends, my health and God's blessings, every day is my Best Day!

-ARTE MORENO
Owner, Los Angeles Angels of Anaheim

The Best Day is every morning that I wake up before the sunrise to go row, I thank God for my health and the first breath of a new day. My other Best Day was medaling at the Nationals in the Lightweight 4. Walking up to the stand I realized how blessed I was for the teammates that had become my best friends. And for my coach, Christy Shaver, who taught me what it was to row with heart and passion.

"No Regrets."

-JILL AUSTIN

Rower; Loyola Marymount University; Singles Rower

The Best Day of my life was probably the day I got married to my wife Linda. We have been married 22 years and our marriage now is as strong as ever. She has blessed me with two lovely and healthy children.

-TOMMY BOWDEN

Head Football Coach, Clemson University, 1998 USA Champion
& Coach of the year, 2X ACC Coach of the Year

Concerning my Best Day, I would have to make it plural. My
Best Days have been the birthdays of my children.

-MIKE DAVIS
Head Basketball Coach, Indiana University, UAB, Texas Southern,3X SWAC
Coach of the Year

My Best Days was when Cal beat Stanford on "The Play". In 1982, Stanford made a field goal late in the game to go up 20-19 against us. Calvin Moen got the kickoff, and as Stanford's defense came at him, Calvin started our "grab ass" play of keep away with lateral passes. The Stanford Band came on the field while the play was still live. After multiple passes, Moen got the ball again, ran over Stanford's trombone player to score the winning touchdown. I designed the play and I was so proud.

-JOE KAPP

NFL Player, BC Lions; Minnesota Vikings, 1969 Pro Bowl,
Coach; University of California.

I have never had a Bad Day! I attack each day with a positive attitude and hopefully my enthusiasm will rub off on the people I'm around. I try to do something for someone that could never re-pay me every day. If I did have to pick a favorite it would have been October 22, 2016. I am the Head Football Coach at Middle Tennessee State University and we were playing the University of Missouri at their home. My son, Brent Stockstill, is my Quarterback and he led us to an upset win, 51-45 by throwing for 4 touchdowns. His leadership and toughness led us to victory! I love my family and to watch my son play that day was a memory I will always cherish.

-RICK STOCKSTILL
Head Football Coach Middle Tennessee State University

I don't really have a "Best Day" story for you. Most of my days are great days, so I find it difficult to come up with one. I am a big fan of Lance Armstrong and one of his quotes aptly describes my life. He says, "Now, I only have good days and great days." (He was speaking about his life after surviving cancer and beating the odds). So, at the worst, I have good days even when the outcome isn't what I want it to be. I have been so blessed and have so much to appreciate and be grateful for, regardless of successes or failures throughout the day.

-MARY HEGARTY
Head Coach Women's Basketball, Long Beach State

The most exciting day of my life was when I met my wife and married her 6 weeks later. That was 52 years ago.

-ANDY GRANATELLI

International Motorsports Hall of Fame,
Motorsports Hall of Fame of America

The days I made it to the big leagues. That opening day, with all those people yelling.

-MARK FIDRYCH

MLB player; Detroit Tigers, 2X All-Star, 1976 Rookie of the Year

Personally, my Best Day was when my wife Tami and I planned to adopt one child from Haiti. But, when we met his four siblings, we opened our hearts and home to all five of them.

As for football, I had so many games and moments it is hard to single out one. I do say, being elected to the Pro Bowl in 1968 was a highlight.

-KERMIT ALEXANDER

NFL Defensive Back, San Francisco 49ers, LA Rams, Philadelphia Eagles, 1969 Pro Bowl

My wife and I will be married 52 years come this January 1997. Perhaps that was my Best Day.

-JOHNNY PESKY

MLB player; Boston Red Sox, Detroit Tigers, Washington Senators, 1946 All-Star, MLB Manager, Boston Red Sox

My Best Day was extended over the weekend through Monday, 1976 when our unheralded University of Virginia team made its first trip to the ACC Tournament finals. Not only did they go up against Dean Smith and a Tar Heel team that included four Olympic players, they won the game. At the time, my wife, Ann Holland, was in the hospital awaiting the birth of our second child. Pregnancy complications had required her to spend the month in the hospital close to the blood bank and operating room. On Monday the doctors delivered our second daughter, Ann-Michael, to complete a very long day that stretched from Saturday night to Monday morning (not much over 24 hours).

-TERRY HOLLAND

Head Basketball Coach, Director of Athletics,
University of Virginia, 1980 NIT Championship

My Best Day was winning the World Championship in 1981. It was a culmination of hard work and determination over the years.

-RON CEY
Professional Baseball Player, LA Dodgers and Chicago Cubs,
6X All-Star, 1981 World Series MVP

My Best Day, I had 5 hits and 2 home runs against the San Francisco Giants or 2 home runs and 3 RBI's against Sandy Koufax in 4-3 Cubs victory over the Los Angeles Dodgers.

-GEORGE ALTMAN

MLB Outfielder, Chicago Cub, St. Louis Cardinals,
New York Mets, 3X All-Star

My Best Day was the day that Joe Germaine, our QB at Ohio State led us to a two-minute drill come-from-behind victory (1:41 seconds left in the 4th quarter) over Arizona State in the 1997 Rose Bowl. Lastly, my parents and all my best friends were at the game as my guests, which was the frosting on the cake for me!

-WALT HARRIS

Head Football Coach, Pittsburg, Stanford University,
Ohio State Quarterback Coach, 2004 Big East Championship,
2X Big East Coach of the Year

My Best Day was August 25, 1958! That was the day I married my wife, Beverly. We will celebrate 46 years of marriage this August. During this time, she has been my lover, my best friend, my biggest fan, and booster. She has given me sound advice without nagging and a shoulder to lean on when needed. She has been a loving and doting mother and has never complained about the time spent with our three children or as she says, her "high-maintenance husband." She is one in a million and not only was August 25 my best day; but Beverly is "the best thing to ever happen to me."

-JUD HEATHCOTE

Head Basketball Coach, Montana, Michigan State University,
1979 NCAA Division Champion, 1990 NABC Coach of the Year,
College Hall of Fame

I have been blessed/lucky:

1. First round draft pick at 19-years old with the Milwaukee Bucks.

2. Breaking UCLA's 88 game win streak while playing at Notre Dame.

3. The day Bernie Bickerstaff asked me to be first assistant coach, along with division of player personnel.

-GARY BROKAW

NBA Player, Milwaukee Bucks, Cleveland Cavaliers,
Buffalo Braves, Assistant Basketball Coach, Charlotte Bobcats,
Head Coach Toronto Raptors

My Best Day was the 2013 Wild Card game against the Reds, I
can still feel the energy from the night.

-NEIL WALKER

MLB 2nd Basemen, Pittsburg Pirates,
2014 Silver Slugger Award

My Best Day for over fifty (50) years was being a part of my teammates Loyola NCAA Basketball Championship. What makes it standout was coming from 15 points down to win in overtime. After those fifty years, I changed my mind, it was the day Loyola met Mississippi State in the NCAA tournament back in 1963. What made that the best day is that it broke a major barrier in not only college basketball but in America. It was the first time a deep south white college team played against black ball players. Because of that game integration had a much easier task. I feel proud that we played a part of American History.

I guess the 3rd Best Day was when I hit the longest shot in basketball history at the time to lead the Indiana Pacers to 117-116 victory over Dallas. It was 88 feet in American Basketball Association (ABA) contest in 1967.

-JERRY HARKNESS
NBA Point Guard, New York Knicks, Indiana Pacers,
1963 NCAA Championship

Wow! Mark, reading your story is very inspirational and amazing of what you have been through.

My Best Days starts every morning reading the Words of God and Praying to God every day. Believing and trusting in God and try to make a difference in some one's life, big or small and keeping a positive attitude.

-ALFRED ANDERSON
NFL Running Back, Minnesota Vikings

There have been many "great" days in my life. The day I was married to my wife, Laurie, even though I was too young (21) to realize how great it was, and the days each of my two sons were born. However, the "best" day was the day I realized I had a one-on-one everlasting relationship with my Lord Jesus Christ. I am forever grateful for that peace and stability in my life.

-CHAN GAILEY

Head Football Coach, Georgia Tech Athletic University,
NFL Head Coach Dallas Cowboys, Buffalo Bills,
Offensive Coordinator Assistant NY Jets

My Best Day was when my wife, Patsy, and I got married on June 1, 1958. I owe so much of my success to her. She has been a great partner for me.

-EDDIE SUTTON

Head Basketball Coach, Creighton, Arkansas, Kentucky,
Oklahoma State University, 1978 & 1986 AP
National Coach of the Year

I have picked a day that was a tribute to me by the Los Angeles Kings for my 25th anniversary with the team. The tribute was held on January 31, 1998 at the great Western Forum and while it was great for me to hear words of praise and receive many thoughtful gifts, the uppermost thought in my mind was that the most satisfying factor to me was longevity. Radio and television is not known for stability among "on-air" personalities and to me the fact that I had spent 25 years in one job in the second largest media market in the United States was cause for much personal satisfaction.

To be able to share that moment with family, friends and fans would qualify; that was my Best Day.

-BOB MILLER

Play-By-Play Announcer, Los Angeles Kings, Foster Hewit Memorial Award from Hockey Hall of Fame, LA Kings Hall of Fame

The first time the coach told us to take off our shirts and start screaming was my Best Day. I didn't know what to do, everyone was a wild bunch! Everyone screaming and doing cheers? I was, like, OK!!

-FROSTEE RUCKER

USC Trojan Football, NFL Defensive End, Arizona Cardinals, Cleveland Browns, Cincinnati Bengals

Basketball has been very good to me and I've had many thrilling and exciting times. However, the Best Day by far was in 1956 when as a member of the Philadelphia Warriors, we won the NBA Championship. This surpasses all individual honors.

-PAUL ARIZIN

Hall of Fame NBA Player, Philadelphia Warriors,
3X All-NBA Team, 1952 All-Star MVP

Professionally--1950 Championship game;
Personally-the day I met Bev.

-OTTO GRAHAM
Hall of Fame NFL Player, Cleveland Browns,
4X AFC Champion, 3X NFL Champion, 5X Pro Bowler

My Best Day would have to be Valentine's Day 1964. This was the day I married my lovely wife Rose.

-NOLAN RICHARDSON

Head Basketball Coach, Western Texas College, Tulsa,
University of Arkansas, 1994 NCAA D1 Champions,
2000 SEC Tournament Champions.

Thanksgiving Day game versus the Cardinals.

-CLIFF HARRIS

Professional Football Player, Dallas Cowboys,
3X Pac-12 Champion, University of Oregon

My Best Day? I don't even have to think twice about it. You'd probably think with the events I cover, the cities I visit and the extraordinary people I have the privilege to meet that one of those areas would involve a "best day."

Not even close…it was June 3, 1987…the day my daughter was born! All five pounds, fifteen ounces of her. My wife, another couple and I were at a Beach Boys concert the previous night…it must have been the "Good Vibrations" that hastened my "Little Surfer Girl" to be born two weeks early. The best part was that she was born at 6:30 P.M., exactly 31 years to the minute after I was born.

That's right, she was born on MY birthday, and I tell her to this day that she's the "gift that keeps on TAKING!!" It drives my wife nuts every year trying to have a separate birthday event for both of us…but I tried to quit celebrating them years ago (or at least quit counting!). To this day she is the light of my life and her birth, by far, my Best Day.

-BRAD NESSLER

ESPN sportscaster

My finest hours were being part of the two NCAA Championship teams. Those two championship games brought me great satisfaction.

-GAIL GOODRICH

Hall of Fame NBA Player, Los Angeles Lakers, Phoenix Suns,
New Orleans Jazz, 1972 NBA Champion, 5X NBA All-Star,
2006 College Basketball Hall of Fame, UCLA

My Best Day professionally was Super Bowl XXXIV, followed by the day I was named head coach of the Rams, and then the day I won my first regular season game.

-MIKE MARTZ

Head Football Coach, St. Louis Rams, San Diego Fleet; Assistant Football Coach Detroit Lions, San Francisco 49ers, Chicago Bears; Super Bowl XXXIV Champion.

Each day is a Best Day as long as you have your health and don't have to fly or listen to commercials by politicians.

When I awakened after triple by-pass rates high in my Best Day category.

-BEANO COOK
ESPN sportscaster

Today! Every day is a Best Day for me.

-WAYNE GRETZKY

Pro Hockey Hall of Fame, Edmonton Oilers, LA Kings, St. Louis Blues, New York Rangers. "The Great One", 4X NHL Stanley Cup winner

Happiest day was victory in Super Bowl VI, had a pretty good game also. Best game--Pittsburg over Chicago 1970 or 1971?

-BOB LILLY

Pro Hall of Fame NFL Player, Dallas Cowboys, 11x Pro Bowler,
7 X First Team All-Pro, 2X NFL Champion,
Super Bowl VI Champion, College Hall of Fame

My most memorable day--to me--was against the Saints, all three of my children were in the stands at the Coliseum with my wife. She would take all three to one game each year. That day I caught three passes for three touchdowns. It was a big thrill for me to have all my family in the stands that day.

-JACK SNOW

NFL Player, Los Angeles Rams, 1967 Pro Bowler

My Best Day, that is easy: the birth of my son, Philip, on August 2, 1981. It was truly being a part of a miracle--it was being given the greatest title one can receive--PARENT.

-PHIL MARTELLI

Head Basketball Coach, Saint Joseph's University, Assistant Coach, Michigan
2004 Coach of the Year & Naismith

There have been so many blessed days in my life, and God has been so good to me that it is difficult to choose one. But if pressed to do so, I will say it was June 17, 1961. That was the day I was married to my wife of now more than 43 years, Lin. We met on a blind date and played miniature golf while the proprietor sang hymns in the background. One year later, we wed in an early morning ceremony, in the garden of my parent's home. I was 22 and Lin was 20.

-ROSS PORTER

MLB Announcer, Los Angeles Dodgers

My Best "Professional' Day came on September 17, 1983 when the Chicago White Sox clinched the American League West title with a victory over the Seattle Mariners. I will never forget the excitement of the fans in the Comiskey Park stands that night and the happiness everyone in the champagne-soaked clubhouse shared as they congratulated one another on the championship. My partner, Eddie Einhorn and I purchased the White Sox in 1981 and the 1983 division title was the first championship won by any Chicago sports team since the 1963 Chicago Bears. Despite winning two more division titles with the White Sox and six NBA World Championships with the Chicago Bulls, the first taste of winning in 1983 still rates as my Best Day.

-JERRY REINSDORF
Owner; Chicago White Sox and Chicago Bulls

The Best Day of my football career was when I was enshrined into the NFL Pro Football Hall of Fame in 1978.

-RAY NITSCHKE

Hall of Fame NFL Player, Green Bay Packers, 1964 Pro Bowl, 5X NFL Champion, 2X Super Bowl Champion, 1962 NFL Championship MVP

I am happy to contribute to your wonderful book. My Best Days would have to be the days my two sons were born. Hands down!

-PHILIP KNIGHT
Founder, NIKE, INC.

Outside the day my three children were born and the day my wife said I DO, my Best Day was just last month. After defeating #1 University of Florida, and being part of South Carolina Team this season to the first Final Four, the 1st time in school history, I stood on the floor at Madison Square Garden and shed tears of joys with my wife, 3 children, and my mother.

-FRANK MARTIN

Head Basketball Coach, Kansas State, South Carolina
Basketball, 2010 Big 12 Coach of the Year

I have had a lot of remarkable good days, but I believe the Best Day I ever had was the day I brought major League Baseball back to Milwaukee. I've had some remarkably great days since then but the thrill of returning Major League Baseball to Milwaukee and Wisconsin will always be the ultimate best day for me.

-ALLAN H. "BUD" SELIG

Commissioner of Major League Baseball, Hall of Fame

Each time I wake up makes that moment the Best Day. The blessings of a fun career that covered just about everything I ever wished for...a great wife and five terrific kids...what else can you ask?

-GIL STRATTON

LA Sportscaster & News Anchor, LA Rams Announcer,
Actor; Stalag 17. The Wild One

I probably had my best and worst day of golf on the same day. (although the worst part of it was only for a few minutes.) Standing on the 72nd green of the 2006 Australian PGA Championship, I had a three-foot putt to win the tournament and also claim the PGA Tour of Australia's order of Merit title. Both titles I'd dreamt of winning when I turned pro. Unfortunately, for a few moments I got ahead of myself thinking about victory speeches, etc and forgot to focus on the task at hand. I missed the putt and wanted to dig a very deep hole somewhere and not come out for a while. While signing my scorecard I dropped a few f-bombs under my breath and stewed on what had just happened. Fortunately, my caddy, Wilber, helped me regroup for the sudden death playoff that was about to start. After halving the first three holes with pars against Peter Lonard, I ended up winning by holing a bunker shot for birdie on the fourth extra hole. The relief and excitement I felt when the ball went in was something, I can never fully explain to people who haven't played competitive sports. The party that night was the special part, because my wife, our two kids, my parents, and many of our close friends were there to help celebrate the victory into the wee hours of the following day. If I was by myself it wouldn't have felt the same, because they're the reason I worked so hard for some many years to achieve my dreams.

-NICK O'HERN

Professional Golfer, 2006 Australian PGA Champion

My Best Day in racing which probably would have been my first and only Winston Cup win at North Wilkesboro in 1990, but when thinking of my very Best Day I think of my wedding day…that was my very Best Day!

-BRETT BODINE

NASCAR Professional; 480 Sprint Cup Races, 1990 1st Union 400 Winner

My Best Days were the days my children were born.

-KIM MULKEY

Head Woman's Basketball Coach, Baylor,
1st woman in NCAA history to win a championship as a player,
assistant coach, and head coach.

Every day is my Best Day.

-FRANK GIFFORD

NFL Hall of Fame Half Back/Flanker, New York Giants;
8X Pro Bowler, 1956 NFL Champion, Monday Night Football
Anchor, USC Football Hall of Fame

My personal Best Day was when my daughter was born on
April 11, 1970.

-GARY WILLIAMS

*Head Basketball Coach, Boston College, Ohio State, University of Maryland;
NCAA Division 1 Champions 2002, ACC Coach of the Year 2002, 2010*

Best Athletic Day: Winning my second Olympic Medal in 2000
with my family there to support me and experience the games
with me. I was thrilled to medal again, especially after battling
a chest cold the week of my race.

-XENO MUELLER

Olympic Singles Rower; 1996 Olympic Gold Medalist,
2000 Silver & Gold Medalist

I don't know if I can identify just one (Best Day). I am lucky to have tens, hundreds of them. Our team laughs at me and I call myself a volleyball dork, because I just love this game.

-KARCH KIRALY

1984 &1988 Men's indoor volleyball team gold medalist,
1996 men's beach volleyball gold medalist,
Coach; US Womens' indoor volleyball.

My Best Day is hearing about great success stories like yours. People like you are my heroes as you continue to bounce back from adversity and setbacks.

-STEVE MEDFIELD
Former Head Basketball Coach, Hampton University

The Best Day of my life is when this bad breath, ugly doctor slapped me on the ass with his cold hands and I screamed "What the ____are you doing? I drew my first breath at that time and have been breathing and enjoying life ever since.

-FRED "The Hammer" WILLIAMSON
NFL Defensive Back, Oakland Raiders, KC Chiefs;
Actor "Black Caesar", "Hell up to Harlem" M*A*S*H

My Best Day was when the politicians and money people told me that opening the Newport Aquatic Center would never happen. In 1987 we opened the doors. Thirty years (and counting), 600 plus members, a great summer program for kids, we proved them wrong.

-BILLY WHITFORD

Crew and Outrigger Paddler; director/founder;
Newport Aquatic Center

My Best Day was when the San Francisco 49ers beat the New York Giants 39-38 in the NFC 2002 first round playoffs.

-JIM MORA JR.

Head Football Coach, Atlanta Falcons, Seattle Seahawks;
Head Coach UCLA, Pac-12 Division Champions, 2012

My Best Day has always been coaching college football--players, preparation, planning and "on the field" association with 90 to 100 outstanding young men--game day is special as well.

-JOHN RALSTON

Former NFL Head Coach, Denver Broncos, Assistant Coach Philadelphia Eagles; Former Football coach; Utah, Stanford University and San Jose State; College Football Hall of Fame

I assume you mean my Best Day in broadcasting. It came in the 1969 Winter Olympics at Squaw Valley when the U.S. Hockey Team defeated the Russians for the first time and I also won the gold medal. It was one of the most emotional days I can recall. I have always felt that the 1960 team did not receive enough recognition they accomplished the feat 20 years before the 1980 hockey team won.

-LON SIMMONS

San Francisco MLB Announcer; recipient of the Ford Frick Award

The day I was born.

-CARMEN BASILIO
*Professional Welterweight & Middleweight Boxer; World
Champion Welterweight and
Middleweight divisions, 56 wins, 27 by KO*

Any day I can look back at my Best Days and not so best days and value every moment of my life. In 1958 rookie coach Peter Daland led a small freshman team from USC to victory over the powerful New Haven Swim club at the U.S. Indoor Championships. The title was decided on the final event, the medley relay, in which I swam the backstroke leg (not my stroke). Unexpected wins against great odds make the best days!

-MURRAY ROSE

1956 three-time Olympic Gold Medal Winner;
1960 Olympics, one gold, one silver, one bronze medal

Recently I was given a surprise party at the NHRA Motor Sports Museum with the entire staff of the NHRA Headquarters and national Dragster publication on hand to celebrate my 90th birthday. With no inkling of its arrangement, and taken totally by surprise, the sharing of this occasion with our in-house troops was definitely an example of an endless chain of my Best Day experiences.

-WALLY PARKS

Founder, Chairman, & President, National Hot Rod
Association (NHRA); International Motorsports Hall of Fame
& American Motorsports HOF

The Best Day for me would have to be the days that my children were born. After each birth, I was prouder of that, than after any race.

-STEVE SCOTT

Hall of Fame Track & Field, UC Irvine; Track & Field Coach, College of San Marcos; 1980 Olympic Trails qualifier during US Olympic Boycott

I've been fortunate to have a lot of good days as a sports columnist covering just about every sort of classic in the spectrum; Rose Bowl, Super Bowl, World Series, Kentucky Derby, USC-Notre Dame football, USC-UCLA football game, John Wooden Championships, the Rod Dedeaux Championships, early Lakers with Elgin Baylor and Jerry West as well as the 1972 Lakers and champs with Wilt, West, Gail Goodrich coached by my all-time favorite, Bill Sharman…and so on and so forth for 50 years. I was lucky to be a newspaperman in the 1950's and 1960's when TV was still a baby and newspapers were still the number one communication force. I've also been lucky to win a number of awards that I cherish.

-JOHN HALL

Sportswriter; Los Angeles Times, Orange County Register and Los Angeles Herald; World Boxing Hall of Fame

I have had many Best Days. But one I will always remember is--the day I was in Dean Cromwells' office at USC having just returned home from World War II and Dean said, "Welcome home, Mel."

-MEL PATTON

*2X Olympic Gold Medalist 1948; 1985 Hall of Fame,
USC Track & Field*

I've had many Best Days, but the best day probably began when I received a scholarship to play football and run track for USC in 1952. That was the beginning of several beautiful opportunities for me. It was a thrill to play with and against so many great athletes, plus achieve a wonderful education. After graduation, and a hitch in the military, I went into law enforcement. Eventually I ended up as the Chief United States Probation Officer for the Federal District of Nevada. I've also had a great family life and retirement.

-FRED PIERCE

Football Player & Track; University of Southern California

Every day is an opportunity for a Best Day. The past and the future came together to create the moment we have in life to love one another. The peace and joy that comes from love is what makes every day a Best Day. Hook 'em!

-AUGIE GARRIDO

Head Coach, Cal State Fullerton: 1979,1984,1995
College World Series Champions; Head Coach, University of Texas;
College World Series Champion 2002, 2005

My Best Day was the day I was named the head coach of the Baltimore Ravens. Another memorable day was the Monday night football game versus the Green Bay Packers. I was coaching for the Vikings and our win broke the Packer's 39-game, home-field winning streak!

-BRIAN BILLICK

NFL Player, San Francisco 49ers, Dallas Cowboys, NFL Coach, Baltimore Ravens; Former Minnesota Vikings offensive coordinator, ESPN Announcer

My Best Day is going to be tomorrow!

-TOM GOLA

Hall of Fame NBA Player, Philadelphia Warriors,
New York Knicks; 5X All-Star, 1956 NBA Champion

I wish I had a Best Day. I feel so blessed to have had so many great days in life. If I had one it would probably have to do with my family. My little nephew or niece--perhaps with my parents. Plus, I have a job in which I can come in to contact with all sorts of interesting people--like you and your wife.

-RICH EISEN

ESPN sportscaster; The Rich Eisen Show

My Best Day is when World War II finished in the Pacific--I was able to return to my family and future wife, Mary.

-LOU CARNESECCA

Hall of Fame Head Basketball Coach, St. Johns University; 3X Big East Coach of the Year

Covering the Super Bowl in Miami (one of my favorite cities--lived there for quite some time) for Fox Sports. I was assigned to the Broncos. All of my on-air hits went perfectly and when the game ended, I was on the field amongst the confetti, under a perfect blue moon. I felt very lucky!

-SUZY KOLBER

ESPN Sportscaster

I had some great days, a lot of them. To pick out one would be hard. In the 1942 World Series, 1946 World Series, and 1956-57-58 Series with the New York Yankees.

-ENOS SLAUGHTER

Hall of Fame MLB Player; St Louis Cardinals,
New York Yankees, Milwaukee Braves, 10X All-Star,
4X World Series Champion

Winning Super Bowl IV.

-HANK STRAM

Hall of Fame NFL Head Football Coach, New Orleans Saints,
Kansas City Chiefs, 3X AFL Champion, Winner, Super Bowl IV

My Best Day? After much thought it would be October 30, 1959, when my wife, Dorothea gave me my first-born, Brian. I know that is pretty basic, but I've never had a happier day than that.

-ROGER CARLSON

Sportswriter/Editor; Daily Pilot

Winning the 2017 US Open was my BEST DAY EVER.

-SLOAN STEPHENS
6 WTA Singles Titles, 2017 US Open Champion

Winning the World Championship. A veteran player obtains goals, achieves status and money, but the ultimate goal is to win a championship.

-DARREN DAULTON

MLB Player; Philadelphia Phillies, Florida Marlins,
3X All-Star, 1997 World Series Champion

1. Orange Bowl 1963 I was credited with 31 tackles in a 17-0 win over Oklahoma.

2. Super Bowl VI, a 24-3 win over the Miami Dolphins.

-LEE ROY JORDAN

NFL Player; Dallas Cowboys, Winner Super Bowl VI;
5X Pro Bowler, 1973 NFL Defensive Player of the Year

My Best Day? Every day!

-ERNIE BANKS

Hall of Fame MLB Player, Chicago Cubs, "Mr. Cub";
14X All-Star, 2X NL MVP, Gold Glover Award 1960

I've had lots of Best Days; difficult to pick just one…birth of children and grandchildren…meeting my wife, Mary Ann Montanaro, and being on the 1982 Cardinals when we won game seven of the World Series…many days watching great racehorses and playing great golf courses.

-JIM KAAT

MLB Player; Philadelphia Phillies, New York Yankees,
St. Louis Cardinals; 3X All-Star, 16X Gold Glove Award,
1982 World Series Champion

My Best Day was December 18, 1977. Dallas played Chicago in Dallas for a division playoff game. That particular day our team won, and I had maybe my best game as a pro. I intercepted three passes in route to a 37-7 victory. That represents an NFC record that still stands and helped contribute to the other record I hold; most interceptions in playoff games.

-CHARLIE WATERS
*NFL Player; Dallas Cowboys, 2X Super
Bowl Champion, 3X Pro Bowler*

1. March 20, 1997 NCAA Tournament - Sweet 16 UCLA vs. Iowa State. I was the newly appointed head coach of the Bruins at UCLA, the interim status was removed from my title in February. It was a game I'll never forget as the Bruins played with all their heart and soul to a big win over Iowa 74-73 in overtime and advanced to the Elite Eight.

2. April 3, 1995 NCAA National Championship - WON IT ALL! I was part of the coaching staff at UCLA when we clinched the National Title in 1995. It was like a dream for me to be there and win it all with the Bruins.

3. Chicago Marathon - Running in and completing the Chicago Marathon to finish is something I find pride in my accomplishment. Competing and training for the sake of personal achievement, this realized in the discipline and satisfaction that I gained from participating in this type of an event to the finish.

-STEVE LAVIN

Former Head Basketball Coach, UCLA, St. John's;
Sports Announcer; 1997 Pac-10 Championship,
2001 Pac-10 Coach of the Year

Being put into the Pro Football Hall of Fame and being picked as MVP of 1962, Player of the Year.

-JIM TAYLOR

Hall of Fame NFL Player, Green Bay Packers, New Orleans Saints, 5X Pro Bowler, 4X NFL Champion, Super Bowl I Champion

I found my Best Day years ago - in a book titled *The Precious Present*. Simply put, my precious present, my best day occurs every day of my life for each one is unique unto itself and can never be duplicated.

-DAVID ODOM

Head Basketball Coach, Wake Forest, South Carolina
University, 3X NIT Championship, 2004 SEC Coach of the Year,
3X ACC Coach of the Year

My Best Day without a doubt was January 22, 1984 the day my daughter, Courtney was born. I have accomplished a lot in my lifetime, but I cherish most my family.

-JEFF RULAND

NBA Player, Washington Bullets, Detroit Pistons,
Head Basketball Coach, Iona College; 2X NBA All-Star,
1982 NBA All-Rookie First Team

My Best Day is when I learned my 36-year old son was clear on his first radiation x-ray after his operation for papillary cancer.

-JERRY PIMM

Head Basketball Coach, Utah, University of California, Santa Barbara; 4X Sweet 16 and 3X NIT Playoffs

I would say that my Best Day was August 25, 1963. That was the day I married my childhood sweetheart, Judy McNamara. I began dating her when she was 12-years old and I was 14-years old. We have been married for 56 years.

-DONNIE WALSH

NBA President, Indiana Pacers

First day in the Big Leagues- all my dreams come true.

-BRONSON ARROYO

MLB Pitcher, Boston Red Sox, Pittsburg Pirates, Reds, Diamond Backs

The Sunday of the 1990 LPGA Championship as my Best Day as a professional. It was my first and only major win on tour to this date. I'll never forget the crowds cheering me on at every green and the chills that it gave me.

-BETH DANIEL
LPGA Golfer; 2000 World Golf Hall of Fame,
33 LPGA Tour wins

Athletically speaking, beating Golden State in 1976 to advance to the NBA finals was my biggest day or Best Day. When the Suns won that seventh game to earn a spot in the finals versus Boston, I was on top of the world.

-DICK VAN ARSDALE

NBA Player, New York Knicks, Phoenix Suns, Coach, Phoenix Suns; 3X NBA All-Star, 1966 NBA All-Rookie First Team

My Best Days were to have been able to play in three NBA All-Star Games but playing in the Indiana High School Championship game in 1965 was also a thrill.

-TOM VAN ARSDALE

NBA Player; Detroit Pistons, Philadelphia 76ers, Phoenix Suns, 3X NBA All-Star, 1966 NBA All-Rookie First Team

Probably my Best Day in sports was January 2, 1963 the Rose Bowl Game in front of 101,000 in Pasadena. It was my first network assignment as a play-by-play for NBC radio. USC 42 - Wisconsin 37...a game rated as perhaps the best in Rose Bowl history. Little did I realize that three-years later I would be living and working in Los Angeles as the voice of the "Trojans." I've been a sports announcer for 55 years and I'm in the Southern California Sportscasters Hall of Fame, so I've been blessed with many Best Days.

-MIKE WALDEN

Hall of Fame Sports Announcer

Personally, as an athlete: Scoring the first and then the winning run in an eight-run final inning victory to overcome a seven-run deficit in a league championship game…way back in 1973 as a senior in high school.

Personally, as a parent: watching any sporting event in which my three children are involved.

Personally, as the sports information director at USC: Privilege since 1979 of being able to come to work every day at Heritage Hall and provide a service to all the athletes, coaches, and staff who make the USC Athletic Department the special place that it is.

-TIM TESSALONE
USC Sports Information Director

As walk-on quarterback at USC it was only a dream to ever play for the Trojans. In fact, when I first walked on, the QB Coach, Paul Hackett, specifically told me USC recruited the best players in the country and that I would never play. He told me as long as I understood that point, I was welcome to be on the team.

One Best Day was the day (about three-years later) that same Paul Hackett took me out to lunch prior to a Spring practice session my senior year and told me I would be USC's starting quarterback in the Fall (1980). I had beaten out the competition and earned the starting position. What a thrill to go from a complete nobody to the starting quarterback at one of the most prestigious college football schools in the Country. I was on cloud nine for a week.

-GORDON ADAMS

Football Player, Corsairs, Newport Harbor High School,
University of Southern California

My Best Day was the day my son was born. I was actually in Atlanta, Georgia at the Super Bowl-away from home-when he decided to debut into this world several weeks early. My husband was there, thank goodness, but that was the best news to hear for all-I was on the air working four days later at Super Bowl XXXIV!

-ANDREA KREMER
ESPN Sportscaster

Many great memories of many great wins, but that feeling is fleeting, and in the big picture, not very relevant. Notre Dame beats Alabama in the Sugar Bowl to win the National Championship...Notre Dame stops Southern Cal and Anthony Davis, Tulane upsets LSU...Colts beat the Forty-Niners. Many games-many years, but not my BEST day. My best day has come from my family. If I had to single one out it would be the day my daughter, who was told she was not good enough or smart enough to succeed, graduated from law school. She didn't prove them all wrong, but she made them realize toughness, perseverance and determination cannot be gauged or tested on paper. It's not about talent or smarts; it's about focus and the will to succeed.

-GREG BLACHE

NFL Assistant Coach; Green Bay Packers, Indianapolis Colts, Chicago Bears, Washington Redskins

I'm not sure if you were able to watch our game two weekends ago versus the UCLA Bruins, it really doesn't rank up there with my wedding day or the births of my children, but as for my most recent Best Day it sure qualifies.

-PETE CARROLL

Former Head Football Coach; University of Southern California;
Current NFL Head Coach, Seattle Seahawks, 2003 &
2004 National Championships, Winner, Super Bowl XLVIII

If I had to narrow it down, it would be in 1996 after winning my first gold medal. After I received my medal, I took it over to my dad and gave him a hug while he was holding a picture of my deceased mother. After my hug with him I went to my sister, Maeola, and gave her my medal. I have always thought she deserved to have been an Olympian.

-RUTHIE BOLTON

Hall of Fame Women's Basketball Player; Sacramento Monarchs, 2 Olympic Gold Medals

Being with my husband and kids and team certainly gives me the highs, the lows, and the middle--day in and day out. To zero in on my basketball life, my best day would be the day we beat Louisiana Tech to qualify for the Final Four. I had it all. My family was in the stands, my team had achieved something no other Penn State women's basketball team had achieved, and we did something people said we could not do.

-RENE PORTLAND

3X National Champion Player, Immaculata; Professional Women's Head Basketball Coach, Colorado, Penn State

My Best Day is every day because it's the gift of life that God
has given us.

-BRIAN KELLY

NFL Player, Tampa Bay Buccaneers, Detroit Lions,
Super Bowl XXXVII Championship

With regards to my storied baseball career, if the reader is a baseball fan the answer is obvious. It would be the October day in 1977 when I hit three home runs on three successive pitches in the World Series, taking the New York Yankees to the championship and winning the Most Valuable Player Award. I would like to pass along a thought-provoking quote, "unless you try to do something beyond what you have already mastered, you will never grow." I truly believe that my best day is yet to come and hope that you will strive to make every day your Best Day.

-REGGIE JACKSON

Hall of Fame MLB Player, Kansas City/ Oakland Athletics, New York Yankees, Anaheim Angels, Oakland A's, 14X All-Star, 5X World Series Champion, 2X World Series MVP

It was September 4, 1983 and the Los Angeles Rams' debut for Coach John Robinson and first-round draft pick Eric Dickerson. It was also my first game as the team's public relations director. Appropriately, we were in New York, my hometown, playing the Giants. What a thrill, to be in the tunnel as the Rams' starting offense—Vince Ferragamo, Jackie Slater, Dennis Harrah and Dickerson-was introduced. And what a thrill it was to be on the sideline near the end of the game, standing next to the great warrior Jack Youngblood as the seconds evaporated on the game clock. Los Angeles 16, New York 6. Vinnie threw a pair of touchdown passes and Eric ran for the first 91 yards of his Hall of Fame career. Quite a day, indeed.

-PETE DONOVAN

LA Rams; Director of Public Relations

January 6, 1979 the day I got married to Sue.

-CRAIG STADLER
Professional Golfer, 1982 Masters Winner, USC Hall of Fame

My Best Day as far as USC goes was being inducted into the USC Sports Hall of Fame, this was May 3, 2002.

-STEVE KEMP

MLB Player, Detroit Tigers, Chicago White Sox,
New York Yankees, 1979 All-Star

My Best Days:

1) Getting drafted by the Detroit Lions
2) My first start as a Detroit Lion
3) My Best Day ever was when Lomas Brown spoke on Thanksgiving Day with the story on when I got hurt.

-MIKE UTLEY
NFL Guard, Detroit Lions, Walter Camp Man of the Year, 2006

I would have to say my Best Day was the day my son was born.

-NICK PRICE

Professional Golfer; 1992 & 1994 PGA Champion,
1994 Open Champion

Remembering the "good days" can sometimes help us get through the tougher ones. As far as my "Best Days" it may be difficult to pinpoint one. However, there are definitely three that stand out in my mind:

1. The day I married my wife Cindy.
2. The day my daughter Lauren was born.
3. The day my son Tyler was born.

-BILL SELF

Head Basketball Coach, University of Kansas, NCAA Champion 2008, John Wooden Legends of Coaches Award 2013

I believe the Best Day of my life was April 1, 1963 when a beautiful baby girl was born to Connie and Dale Brown by the name of Robyn.

-DALE BROWN

Hall of Fame Head Basketball Coach,
Louisiana State University

There are many that come to mind, however, the day I was chosen as basketball coach at USC in 1966. This enabled me to return to my Alma Mater.

-BOB BOYD

Hall of Fame Head Basketball Coach, University of Southern California; Pac-12 Men's Basketball Hall of Honor &USC Basketball Hall of Fame

Passed for 509 yards in one game versus Chicago Bears, 1982.

-VINCE FERRAGAMO

NFL Player; LA Rams, Buffalo Bills, Green Bay Packers,
1976 Sporting News College Football Player of the Year,
1X NFC Champion

My Best Day as a Green Bay Packer was playing in the Championship game in Green Bay after spending five years losing in Los Angeles with the Rams. This was at the end of the 1965 season and I was able to catch a touchdown pass from Bart on a snowy day. Just being a member of a championship team made
it a Best Day.

-CARROLL DALE

Professional Football Player, Los Angeles Rams,
Green Bay Packers; Athletic Director; Clinch Valley College

Every day!!

-JAMAAL WILKES

*NBA Player, Golden State Warriors, Los Angeles Lakers,
LA Clippers, 4X NBA Champion, 3X NBA All-Star,*

I was coaching at Davidson College in a game against East Carolina for the Southern Conference Championship in November 1969. The East Carolina single wing baffled us for a while, and we found ourselves down 7 to 28. We won 42 to 28 in one of the biggest turn-around in the history of championship play. It was in the book of records, at least for a while. That day the players experienced that there is another level within reach. I guess I have known for that next level to be reached in some other games, but none stands out in my mind like the day in Greenville, North Carolina on East Carolina's home field.

-HOMER SMITH

Head Football Coach, Davidson, Pacific,
Army; SoCon Champions 1969

Nothing came close to my best day-- that was winning
Wimbledon on July 1, 1977.

-VIRGINIA WADE

Hall of Fame Professional Tennis Player;
US Open Winner, Australian Open winner, Wimbledon winner

1950 Championship game versus L.A. Rams. I kicked a sixteen-yard field goal in the closing seconds for the game winning points, 30-28.

-LOU GROZA

Hall of Fame NFL Player, Cleveland Browns,
9X Pro Bowler, 5X NFL Field Goal Kicker, 4X NFL Champion

My most memorable experience in golf was winning the 1961 US Open at Oakland Hills Country Club in Birmingham, Michigan.

-GENE LITTLER

Hall of Fame Professional Golfer; 1961 US Open Winner

Every day is the Best Day of my life. Today is the Best Day of my life. You have to seize the moment.

-BILL WALTON

Hall of Fame NBA Player; Portland Trail Blazers,
LA Clippers, Boston Celtics; 2X NBA Champion,
1977 NBA MVP, 2X All-Star; Sports Announcer

Being inducted into the Professional Football Hall of Fame in Canton, Ohio.

-ELROY "Crazy Legs" HIRSCH

*Hall of Fame NFL Player, Chicago Rockets, LA Rams,
3X Pro Bowler, 2X AP 1st Team All-Pro, 1951 NFL Champion*

1st game-coming out the tunnel and seeing my parents in the stands was a Best Day. Recently, the Notre Dame game. Not because of how I had such a great game personally, but it was so special because it was Senior Day. Seeing who was leaving, the tassels around their necks, and their families-and we wanted to win for them. At that point, we didn't know we would be going to the Rose Bowl, so it was special to honor our USC Seniors. We were in such a great position, on a great win streak and we controlled the possibility to go to the Rose Bowl. The entire vibe was amazing.

-ADOREE' JACKSON
USC Wide Receiver/Punt Returner 2014-2017, Tennessee Titans

I would have to say that the day I will never forget was the day I walked out of my doctor's office on a beautiful sunny day in August 1987. She had just confirmed that my husband and I were going to have a baby. My father passed away in June and when I walked out and looked up in the sky, I felt my dad's presence, and the warmth that the "circle of life" goes on.

-CINDY FREDRICK

Head Women's Volleyball Coach, Washington State University

Growing up in Southern California and having a Father who always told me great stories about famous USC athletes, I'd have to say my best day is the day I got accepted with a full athletic scholarship to USC. This did not come easy for I was not the best student in High School. Despite the scholarship offer, I needed a two-year Community College GPA raising my effort to make my "USC-My Best Day" a reality. The dream came true for me and my dad.

-BOB SEAGREN

University of Southern California, Track; 1968 Olympic Gold Medalist, pole vault, USC Hall of Fame

The day we beat Kansas, that was my Best Day.

-JIM BOEHEIM

Hall of Fame Head Basketball Coach, Syracuse,
2003 NCAA National Champions, 2010 Naismith College Coach of the Year

My Best Day is Alumni Day which kicks off the baseball season at UCLA. For 3 years I have enjoyed this day more than any other because I get to visit with my former players who come back to play or watch the alumni game. I love to listen to their laughter that surrounds their slightly exaggerated stories of "yester-year" … and I like telling them how much older they look while I've stayed the same as when they played for me.

-GARY ADAMS

Former Head Baseball Coach, UCI, UCLA, 1973 & 1974 DII National Championship, 1974 DII Coach of the Year,

I competed in several sports on a high level, but I will describe my Best Day as follows:

In 1936, while in London I tore some muscles in my right shoulder and right-side chest. The specialists in England told me that I would never be able to play tennis again. I received the same information while I was seeking a second opinion from the expert doctors in New York. However, within three or four weeks I tried to play. Don Budge and I won four "majors" after the injury and Alice Marble and I won another major defeating Don and Sarah Palfrey in the finals of the U.S. National at Brookline. Nevertheless, my very Best Day has to be when I reached the Finals of the U.S. national Singles against Don in 1938, when he won the "Grand Slam."

-GENE MAKO

Hall of Fame Tennis Player; 1937 & 1938 Wimbledon
Champion-Doubles, 1936 & 1938 US Open Doubles Champion

I have been coaching youth volleyball now in the Orange County, CA area for over 15 years. I have coached at five different high schools, boys and girls club and was volunteer assistant at the University of California, Irvine. There have been some amazing matches I have been involved with, both on the good side and bad side of the outcome. I have many wonderful memories of these matches and the boys and girls who I have coached over the years. Some have graduated, got married and even had children of their own since I have touched their lives on the volleyball court. The relationships I have built with my players over the years is what I cherish most about coaching these young adults. However, through all my coaching experiences my Best Day came on July 2nd, 2009.

After starting practice in the fall of 2008 with the 14 and under girls for Orange County Volleyball Club, four months later my team of 14 Blue Team was established. Everything was building up to the largest annual youth sporting event in the world, the Volleyball Festival in Phoenix, AZ. This is where over 8,000 girls from ages 12-18 would participate in a week long tournament that would finish in the US Airways Center where the NBA Team, The Phoenix Suns, play.

The OCVBC 14 Blue team played well all week winning all of their matches and losing only one game. After beating the reigning champs, Puerto Rico, in the round before the quarter-finals, our starting opposite right side player tore some ligaments in her ankle in a freak accident celebrating with her teammates. Although we were playing well, our chances to teach our goal looked a little dim. She was one of our leaders on and off the court and the girls were crushed. All of this said, the other ten girls really stepped up and played with a lot of heart to beat two very good teams to reach the Finals. Out of 103 teams, only one more stood in our way to the title.

I remember the day like it was yesterday. What we had for breakfast, walking into the arena for the first time, and seeing the expressions on the girls faces when I took them on the floor where we would play before we went to the locker room for our pre-game talk. They actually were able to change and get ready in the players locker room. When we walked in, they had their names on place cards over each locker. It was pretty exciting for 13 and 14-year-old girls. Heck, it was pretty exciting for a 39-year old coach.

As we were warming up, I remember how nervous I was. I thought to myself if I was this nervous, how were the girls feeling? We warmed up, and I gave my talk, so we were ready to go. The format was 2 out of 3. The first two games were played to 25 and the third one, if necessary, was played to 15 points, having to win by two. The first game was a blur. The girls were scared, nervous and were like deer in head lights. I tried everything, but it didn't matter. We ended up losing that first game pretty bad. As I was turning in my lineup, I looked over and saw one of my Captains getting into the faces of the other girls. She was fired up wanted to light a fire under the girls she has battled with all year long. She was not about to go down this way and rallied her teammates to a

dominating win in game two. It came down to the third and
final game. It went back and forth. I remembered the crowd
getting louder and louder. It seemed everyone was standing
from about 12-12 on. Past 15 we went. We had match point,
then they had it. Momentum kept switching sides. Then finally
at 21-20, we dug a driven ball perfectly to the setter where she
set out middle blocker and she put the ball away. As the girls
dog piled in the center of the court, I stood there with my
assistant coach just watching the joy and excitement that these
girls have worked so hard for the last ten months. I was so
proud of these girls. As I hugged the girls, parents, and other
coaches from our club, I remember tears running down my face.
During my coaching career, this was by far my Best Day.

-SCOTT BRUCE

Assistant Coach, UCI; Head Coach OCVBC

1. The day I was picked for my high school basketball team.
2. Being picked for the basketball Hall of Fame in 1972.
3. The day the Syracuse Nationals won the NBA Championship in 1955.

-DOLPH SCHAYES

Hall of Fame NBA Player; New York Knicks, 1955
NBA Champion, 12X All-Star, NBA Coach
Philadelphia 76ers, Buffalo Braves

I would have to say my Best Day was winning the 1998 Buick Invitational Golf Tournament. I was born and raised in San Diego and it was always a dream of mine to win at home on the Torrey Pines Golf Course. I hadn't won on the PGA Tour in five years and wasn't doing all that great in the first two rounds. Stan Humphries, the San Diego Charger Quarterback, was caddying for me, which was a lot of fun, and when I started making birdies it got even more fun. I was doing great in the third round, but we had a rain delay and had to come back Sunday afternoon to finish the third round which would be our last round. It came down to just one player who could tie me, and Skip Kendall made a ten-foot putt to force the playoff. I was really nervous on my putt and thought I had to make it to force another hole in the playoff. I went through my normal routine and knocked it in. Then I got a great surprise when Skip's putt lipped out and I was the winner.

-SCOTT SIMPSON
Professional Golfer; 1987 US Open Champion, 17 Tour wins

In respect to sports, my Best Day was actually a game in which my team lost the 1967 UCLA-USC game 20-21. The significance of the game for me is what it represented rather than the result. For me and my senior teammates, it was the opportunity to play for the national championship in our hometown (we have never lost a game on California soil). The goal of a national championship had been the primary motivator for us for the prior two years, in which we had finished in the top five in the Country. Granted, we did not achieve our goal; more important, we actually positioned ourselves to play for the number one ranking. Given how many people play the college football game and participate in many losing games, we had the good fortune to only lose five out of thirty and again, make it to a Saturday afternoon in which we missed by only one point. Considering all of the times one can play and lose, we were fortunate, and my time playing the game is a wonderful lifetime memory.

-GARY BEBAN

Heisman Trophy Winner; UCLA, NFL Player Washington Redskins

The day J.D. Morgan hired me was very special. I wanted to beat USC and I knew I couldn't with my teams at Occidental College. I promised J.D. it would happen in two years. I recruited the people USC didn't have my first year--we beat them the second year with ease. Very close to my greatest day would be my Trojan team that went to Austin, Texas for the 1992 NCAA Championship that covered four days. The competition was outstanding, but our very small group was unbelievable!

-JIM BUSH

Hall of Fame Track Coach, UCLA and USC

WHAT A GREAT CONCEPT!!

Looking back over my career, I have had MANY Best Days! I was very fortunate. If I had to say one, it would be the opening game with the Lakers. The reason being, I didn't attend the University of Northern Colorado in hopes I would play professional basketball, I thought I was already a professional; the school was giving me a scholarship. Upon graduating, I was able to try out for various NBA teams, and made the Lakers roster. Going through the warmups of the first game of the regular season, was a dream come true. I had made the NBA! The short period of time I was with the Lakers, I learned things that I still live by arriving 15 minutes early is on time, the team is the most important thing and work harder than anyone else.

I wish you the BEST OF LUCK with your book, MAKE IT A GREAT DAY!

-MIKE HIGGINS

NBA Power Forward, LA Lakers, Denver Nuggets, Sacramento Kings

I was a certified, confirmed bachelor. Life had been kind but incomplete. In 1999 I crossed paths with someone I had met 30 years earlier. Elaine was the sister of my former teammate, Clifford Branch, who came over to my house and I asked about his sister. I asked her to be my date in Las Vegas at a 50th birthday party for a former teammate. She looked great and I actually tried to get her to elope with me in Las Vegas. I offered her my Super Bowl ring as a wedding ring! She turned me down, but we dated for two years. On June 30, 2001 we married in Houston, Texas. I was 52-years old and had never been married. I am a stroke patient. Since our marriage, I am no longer on high blood pressure medicine. Elaine, my wife, is a keeper and I love her dearly. To make our best days the absolute best we enjoy visits from our children John and Shane, Tyler and Danielle...God is good!

-CLARENCE DAVIS

NFL Player, Oakland Raiders, Super Bowl XI Champion. USC Hall of Fame

I'd have to say my Best Day was the day I announced I was staying in school for one more year.

-RICKY WILLIAMS

NFL Player, New Orleans Saints, Miami Dolphins,
Baltimore Ravens, 2002 Pro Bowl MVP, 2X Jim Brown Trophy,
Heisman Trophy Winner- University of Texas

We have been blessed with so many wonderful days, it is nearly impossible to single one out above others. We remain grateful for our days and certainly look forward to the gift of today.

-HERB SENDEK

Head Basketball Coach, Miami Ohio, North Carolina State, Arizona State, 1995 MAC Regional Championship, 2010 Pac-10 Coach of the Year

My Best Day was being drafted by the Atlanta Falcons! Who would have thought that a kid from Tabor College would play nine years in the NFL. I have a pretty good career as well. I am so blessed.

-ROLLAND LAWRENCE
Cornerback; Atlanta Falcons, 1X All-Pro, 1977 Pro Bowl

My biggest and Best Day was a visit to a hospital for an appendix operation. It was at this hospital that I met my wife and we have shared our lives together ever since (50 years).

-BOBBY ROSS

NFL Coach, San Diego Chargers, Detroit Lions, 1994 AFC Champions, Head Football Coach, Georgia Tech, Army; 1990 National Championship, 1990 Coach of the Year

My Best Day is today because there is always a chance that something great will happen. My next Best Day? Tomorrow of course.

-TOM BRENNAN

Head Basketball Coach, University of Vermont

My Best Day was July 9, 1976 when I no hit the Expos. Didn't get to sleep until 6:00 A.M. A close second was the day we clinched the Central Division Championships in my rookie year as manager, 1997.

-LARRY DIERKER

MLB Player; Houston Colts/Astros, St Louis Cardinals, 2X All-Star, MLB Manager; Houston Astros, 1998 NL Manager of the Year

I am indeed fortunate that I can say on balance I have experienced many more good days in my life than bad. If I had to pick my best day, aside from the birth of my daughter and other family related days, I would say that my Best Day was when I was picked by my graduate school classmates to speak for them at our graduation from the USC School of Physical Therapy.

One is not chosen for this honor because you are Valedictorian or have the highest GPA or the like. I was chosen by my classmates. As we were nearing the end of our program, an announcement was made that we needed to pick a speaker, and anyone who was interested should write their name on a piece of paper that was being passed around class that day. When I passed it along to the girl sitting next to me, she asked why I didn't place my name on the list. "because I don't want to do it." I said, which she says, "you are going to be our speaker, as she placed my name along about seven or eight of my classmates. A few days later we then got up in front of our class, to make out pitch of how we would do the speech.

"I really don't want to do this". That was my pitch to my classmates. I was afraid that the anticipation and stress of doing the speech would ruin graduation for me. To my dismay, I got more votes that anybody on the first ballot, and it was agreed that a run-off wasn't necessary. I asked my classmates to write down things they thought should be included and leave them in my mailbox. I ended up writing the bulk of it during a long boring lecture class with my anatomy partner and good friend. As he sat across from me we basically wrote the speech, and I had it "in the can" as they say, about a week prior to graduation.

This reduced my stress immensely, I found myself in a quiet room about an hour before the ceremony, putting on some finishing touches, and actually writing the very first lines I would say. When I was called to the podium I felt as if a heavy weight were on my shoulders. I strode to the dais slowly, almost as if stricken. As soon as I began, all of the butterflies went away. It was like when you are playing a sport, and you can't miss, almost like an out of body experience. I don't want to be dramatic, but I literally made them laugh, made them cry, and moved. In the beginning of the speech, I shared a quote. It goes something like, "*Understanding is at times preceded by profound and horrible confusion*". It seemed an apt way to describe a lot of what we went through as PT students. After talking about our shared experiences, and sharing more than a few inside jokes, I closed with, "*Though there is much that I learned from out professors, it was often on of my classmates who rescued me from the depths of profound and horrible confusion.*" As soon as I delivered my last line, I walked off the stage to a standing ovation, returned to my seat and cried,

Clearly an amazing experience, and also one of the Best Days of my life.

-GARY P KONECNE
Physical Therapist, Disabled Ski Instructor, Father, USC School of Physical Therapy 1996

Even though I have been blessed with many Best Days in my basketball career and short life span, the one that clearly stands head and shoulders above the rest is the day of July 19, 1994; the day my daughter Kiara Elizabeth was born into my life forever. After this day; all my other Best Days got even better because now I truly had a reason for them, to share them with my beloved child. Every day I see and speak to Kiara are my Best Days going forward.

-JEROME KERSEY

NBA Player; Portland Trail Blazers, LA Lakers, Seattle Supersonics, Milwaukee Bucks, 1999 NBA Champions Assistant NBA Coach, Milwaukee Bucks

I would have to say that the "Best Day in Pro Football" for me was the day I was able to call my father and say to him "Daddy, I made the team."

My father was playing college football when he learned that he would soon become a young father. He moved back home, enrolled at the local college and got a job. When I became old enough to play, he began to coach me, from Pop Warner through High School. He watched all of my ups and downs, saw me fight through injury and different setbacks. So, it was with great pride that I was able to tell him that I had made the team!

-COURTNEY GRIFFIN
NFL Defensive Back Los Angeles Rams

My Best Rams Day was my rookie year in 1990, my first NFL start! We were playing the San Francisco 49ers and I had my first NFL interception against Joe Montana!

Great Fun!

-PAT TERRELL

NFL Player, LA Rams, NY Jets, Carolina Panthers, Green Bay Packers

My Best Day would have to be when I tore my ACL and NCL in 2009, Green Bay released me, which cost me 1.5 million dollars. Green Bay went on to win the Super Bowl that year.

I got my knee fixed, and was signed by The Giants, won the Super Bowl with them the following year.

I never gave up!

-WILL BLACKMON

NFL Cornerback, Safety; Green Bay Packers, NY Giants, Seattle Seahawks, Jacksonville Jaguars, Washington Redskins, Super Bowl XLVI Champion

My Best Day was when I retired from the NFL in 1985 with no surgeries in 13 years, and I never missed a game or a practice, and I walked away healthy.

-JOE DeLAMIELLEURE

NFL Player, Buffalo Bills, Cleveland Browns, 6X Pro Bowl, NFL 1970's All-Decade Team, Pro Football Hall of Fame

I could never say I had one Best Day. I have had too many perfect days to single out one.

My wedding day is among the most memorable, perfect days I have ever experienced. The birth of my son, Tyler, ranks right up there. My husband, Mark, and I have had some amazing days in Italy, France, and Australia.

But there was one simple day that I often reflect upon with great tenderness. It was a summer day in 2006. I was on an extended maternity leave from ESPN.

I was home with my then-7-month old son, Ty. The weather was brilliant! It was about 78 degrees and sunny with a mild, warm breeze and a few clouds in the sky. Gardening is one of my favorite things to do on such days. So, I put on my gardening gloves, put Ty in his "Exerciser" and we settled into the front yard.

While I dug in the dirt and planted some annuals, Ty played, laughed and gurgled

-MICHELE TAFOYA

Sportscaster, 2002-2008 NBA on ESPN, NBC Sunday Night Football reporter, KQRS Morning Show Co-Host

'

\=

I'm new at an age when any day I can get out of bed is my Best Day. But, reflecting back over the years, I would have to say that my Best-Best Day was the day I first saw my wife-to-be. Well, I really didn't see her, I saw her picture in a yearbook. For at that time I was a first-year law student at the University of Michigan. And not only did I not know any of the girls on campus, having done my undergraduate work elsewhere, but my fellow classmates, most of whom had also done their undergraduate work at other colleges, had even less of a clue. So, I bought a yearbook and went through it, picture-by-picture, until I came across a picture of the prettiest girl I ever saw. Cross referencing the name that went with the picture, "Suzanne Davis", I found she lived in a sorority house and called. However, not knowing who the hell I was, she wouldn't answer the call. Undeterred, I found out her roommate's name and called her. Even dated her to get an introduction to the object of my affections. That was 50 years ago, and Suzanne Davis Sugar for a half century since that "day", My "Best Day"

-BERT SUGAR

Boxing Writer and Sports Authority. Boxing Illustrated Editor, International Boxing Hall of Fame, Ellis Island Medal of Honor

(After winning Silver in 2010 Vancouver Olympics). This is more than redemption than you can ever think from Torino, it's the Best Day of my life.

-JERET "SPEEDY" PETERSON

Olympic Silver Medal, Freestyle Arial's, 2010, National Champion, Gold

My Best Day was the Gold Medal game in Vancouver at the Winter Olympics on February 28th, 2010. It was an overtime game vs. USA and we (Canada) scored to win the game in overtime.

-LINDY RUFF

NHL Left Wing player, Buffalo Sabers, New York Rangers, NHL Coach Florida Panthers, Florida Stars.

Winning the women's USA Gold in Judo was the Best Day of my life.

-KAYLA HARRISON

Judoka, 2012 Gold Medalist, London Olympics, 2016 Gold Medalist, Rio Olympics

Every day is a Best Day, and even if my man shoots 80, I'm happy.

-PETE BENDER
Legendary Golf Caddy

Although marrying my wife Sue Sommer-Kresse was a highlight in my life; ...the "Best Day" was October 11, 1986. It was the birth date of our twin sons Ryan and John.

-JOHN KRESSE

Head Basketball Coach, College of Charleston, Assistant Head Coach St John's, New York Nets, 3X TAAC Coach of the Year, 6 time NAIA Champion, College Basketball Hall of Fame

Winning the Olympic Gold Medal in the men's downhill race in 1998; it was the Best Day of my life!

-JEAN-LUC CRETIER

1998 Nagano Olympic Gold Medalist, Men's Downhill Skiing

While in New York, I worked with inner city kids in Harlem from the Harlem Youth Soccer before a game in 2007 with the Galaxy vs the Rangers. I played a pickup game with some of the local youngsters, and it actually was one of the Best Days since I arrived in America.

-DAVID BECKHAM

European Midfielder; Footballer, Manchester United, Real Madrid. US Professional Soccer, L.A. Galaxy; 2011 MLS Cup Winners. Professional Model,

My Best Day way when my 21 year old son, Sean was born. My 2nd Best Day was when I met my wife Roberta O'Neill!

-KEVIN O'NEILL

Head College Basketball Coach, Marquette, Tennessee, Northwestern, University of Arizona, USC; NBA Assistant Coach; Pistons, Raptors, Pacers

Probably my "Best Day" in broadcasting Kansas Jay Hawk athletics came in 1952 when U had the honor of airing Kansas' win over St. John's of New York from Seattle, giving the Jay Hawks the NCAA Championship.

The "Hawks" were led by Clyde Lovellette, who is still the only player ever to be named tourney MVP and also to have led the nation in scoring.

--MAX FALKENSTEIN
University of Kansas Basketball Sportscaster

My Best Day was the day my husband Scott asked me to marry him! 25 plus years later with 3 sons it is still the best decision I ever made.

-TRACY AUSTIN

Tennis; 1979,1981 US Open Winner, 1980 Wimbledon Winner, Career 351-90

I have three Best Days:

1) The Day my wife Margaret married me
2) The day my daughter Megan came into this world.
3) The day my daughter Molly came into this world.

-JIM McLAUGHLIN

Men's Head Volleyball Coach, USC, Women's Head Volleyball Coach Kansas State, University of Washington, Notre Dame, NCAA 2004 National Coach of the Year, 5X Pac-12 Coach of the Year

My "Best Day" was unequivocally the day the USA Women's Soccer Team defeated Brazil 2-1 in overtime to win the 2004 Olympic Gold Medal.

Keep Kicking!

-APRIL HEINRICHS

Women's National Soccer Team Player 1986-1991, Managed Princeton, University of Maryland, University of Virginia, University of California, Irvine, USA National Team, 1995-2005, USSF Technical Advisor

As a UCLA letterman and two-platoon player for UCLA headman, Henry R. (Red) Sanders, then as now, my Best Day as a 'gutty little Bruin' was and is whenever we beat USC…on the gridiron. I'll take a win over the Trojans on the courts (basketball, tennis, volleyball), n the oval (track; or on the field (baseball, softball, field hockey), but you just can't beat a butting heads pasting of SC between the chalk lines.

-WERNER ESCHER
UCLA Football

I will give you a couple of Best Days. My wedding day and the day I started doing Bills Football in 1960.

-VAN MILLER

Announcer, "the Voice of the Bills", 1999 Greater Buffalo Hall of Fame

I have had the food fortune of having many memorable days in my career as a Horse Trainer. I do not believe that there is one specific great day that I can think of that would be greater than another, but, certainly I think two of the greatest days was when JOHN HENRY won the first running of the Arlington Million and another great day was in 1990, when I was elected to the Racing Hall of Fame. One other memorable moment was when NORTHERN SPUR won the 2 Million Breeder's Cup race in New York. As I mentioned before, there has been several, but I think these have been the best.

-RAND McANALLY

Professional Horse Trainer, Horse Racing Hall of Fame

Having been heavily involved in sports for the past fifty years, many "Best Days" come to mind. Some of the these are from my playing days as a youngster, other as a coach in hockey and baseball. These best days are usually remembered for the thrills of winning big games.

"Best Days" of course, often refer to other areas of life besides sports. These could include marriage, the birth of a child, a Friday evening playing floor hockey, and basketball in a church basement. After, we would go upstairs to a lounge when the youth pastor would give us refreshments along with a short talk. On one such Friday evening, I happened to be listening to what he was saying, He was telling us how Jesus loved each one of us, wanted to take us to heaven when our lives were over. He also invited us to stay after if we wanted to hear more about Jesus. Something inside me urged me to stay and along with another youngster, Christianity was explained to us in a way that we could understand it. It seemed so simple. Jesus loved us so much that He died for us as a sacrifice so that we could have a chance to go to heaven. All we had to do, was ask Him to forgive us for every wrong thing we'd ever done and allow Him to take over our lives. That night I become a Christian.

It didn't seem all that big a deal at the time, but looking back at all that happened since, it was by far the most important day in my life. I can get help handling life's problems through prayer and studying my Bible and when it's all over, I know I'll be on my way to heaven.

-ROGER NEILSON

NHL Coach, Toronto Maple Leafs, Vancouver Canucks, Los Angeles Kings, Philadelphia Flyers

I have been blessed with many, many Best Days. Days with family, friends, and while coaching and playing volleyball. Best Days happen when we plan for each day to be our Best Day.

-MIKE WILTON

Head Volleyball Coach, University of Hawaii, Assistant Coach, BYU

2 Special Days in baseball career, My Major League first base hit, July 5, 1940. Coach with Pittsburg Pirates in 1979- "We are Family"

-AL MONCHAK

MLB Pitcher, Philadelphia Phillies, Coach, Pittsburg Pirates

My Best Day as a New York Giants was in a 1969 game against the Philadelphia Eagles. Had a chance to play against Bob Brown, All-Pro from Nebraska. Made a few good plays I'm proud of!

-MCKINLEY BOSTON

NFL Defensive End, New York Giants, University of Minnesota Athletic Director

My most unforgettable moment came when I rode my first race in July of 1967 at Jong Acres Racetrack in Renton, Washington.

I rode a mare named Roberta H in the first race in the one post position and I won, she paid $87.00 to win. I remember I wasn't nervous until I made the lead then I didn't know what to do. I never thought that would happen and then when I came back after the race my hands were shaking so bad, I couldn't unfasten my chin strap for the win picture.

So that's my story!

-RICHARD CULBERTSON

Jockey

My Best Day in golf was winning the Triple Crown Title in 1977. I won in a playoff with Judy Rankin and JoAnne Carner. It was the first time my parents ever saw me win!

-JANE BLALOCK

Professional Golfer, 27 wins on LPGA, 1969 LPGA Rookie of the Year

My Best Day; winning my first Major League Game

-ED ERAUTT
MLB Pitcher, Cincinnati Reds, St Louis Cardinals,

1. In the second game of the season against Colorado State on the road to Colorado, Idaho trailed at the end of the first quarter 28-0. At that time Idaho was Division 1-AA playing a 1-A opponent. To make a long story short, under the head coach of John L. Smith, the Vandals won by a score of 37-34--what a Best Day!

2. In 1998 the third year in the Big West Conference as a 1-A member, Idaho played archrival Boise State at Boise in the final game of the year--the winner to go on to the Humanitarian Bowl to play Southern Mississippi. The game went into overtime and the Vandals won on a two-point conversion, a great call by a normally conservative coach Chris Tormey. Final overtime score was 36-25 Vandals. Another best day and incidentally Idaho beat Southern Mississippi in the Humanitarian Bowl 42-35!!!

-BOB CURTIS

Sports Announcer, University of Idaho

One Best Day – pinch hitting for Willie McCovey and driving in the tying run-the runner was Willie Mays.

-JOEY AMALFITANO

MLB Second Baseman, New York/San Francisco Giants, Houston Colt 45s, Chicago Cubs, Manager, Chicago Cubs, Coach Los Angeles Dodgers

My Best Day is Baseball- playing in two games of the 1960 World Series for Pittsburgh Pirates against the Yankees in Yankee Stadium and winning both games. Finally won the series on my home run in the 7th game.

-BILL OLDIS

MLB Catcher, Washington Senators, Pittsburg Pirates, Philadelphia Phillies, 1x World Series Champion

My Best Day in baseball would be the moment that David Freese hit the walk-off homer in game 6 of the 2011 World Series. I was with my family and was able to enjoy that moment in all its glory.

-WILLIAM O. DeWITT III
President and CEO, St. Louis Cardinals

My Best Day was in Seattle while playing for the White Sox in 1977. I hit for the cycle. 1st two at bats were doubles. Then a home run, followed by a single. Last at bat manager Bob Lemon told me is to get a hit and to not stop till I reach third. I hit a gapper and made it to third.

-JACK BROHAMER
MLB 2nd & 3rd Baseman, Cleveland Indians, Chicago White Sox, Boston Red Sox

I guess my Best Day, at least more memorable was catching the no-hitter thrown by Jim Bibby against the Oakland A's in 1973. Also, the last game at RFK Stadium in Washington D.C...we had to forfeit against the Yankees in 1971.

-RICH BILLINGS

MLB Catcher/Left Fielder; Washington Senators, Texas Rangers, St. Louis Cardinals

My Best Day was July 11, 2008 when I nearly pitched a complete game shutout at LA in my 1st Major League start… 8 2/3 innings and then a run scored against me. Closer Keven Gregg got the final out and the Marlins and I won the game 3-1.

-CHRIS VOLSTAD

MLB Pitcher, Florida Marlins, Chicago Cubs, Colorado Rockies, Pittsburg Pirates

Breaking the world record in the 400-meter freestyle relay in the 2008 Beijing Olympics. To top it off, I was telling my wife that this is second Best Day of my life, next to my wedding.

-JASON LEZAK

Olympic Swimmer, 2000 Sydney gold- 4X400 Medley & silver
4 X 100 medley; 2004 Athens gold- 4X100 Medley, bronze-100 freestyle,
2008 Beijing-gold 4X100 medley & 4 X100 freestyle, 2012 London-silver
4X100 freestyle

Being able to look up in the stands and see my parents when I went up to bat in my second MLB Ball game.

-JORDAN PACHECO

MLB Baseball Player, Colorado Rockies, Arizona Diamondbacks, Cincinnati Reds

I have had a lot of Best Days-the very best day was 3 hits at
Fenway Park in Boston in 1940.

CARL MILES

MLB Pitcher, Philadelphia Athletics

June 11, 1983 was my Best Day in baseball because I faced off against my hero, Johnny Bench.

I was so nervous, and Johnny knew it by the way my legs were trembling (I was 19 years old). He said, "Kid, just see the ball and swing at it" I did…I struck out. I went 0 for 2 but we won the game. Awesome day.

-GIL REYES

MLB Baseball Catcher, Los Angeles Dodgers, Montreal Expos

When you take a look back on my career, I tore my ACL April 23RD, 2010, during the ACC tournament vs Clemson Tigers. I just knew my career was over, that's how much pain I was in. Long story short, I had surgery and I started rehab immediately. During the process of trying to rebuild my knee, I doubted myself multiple times. I didn't understand why I was chosen to handle a tough situation like the one I was put in. As time moved on, I got stronger and better, happier and mentally stronger. Being able to realize that I would be able to get back on the court again and do what I loved most, was one of the best feelings in the world. Stepping onto the court for practice after being out for a year was one of the Best Moments/Days of my career.

-ALEX MONTGOMERY

WNBA New York Liberty, San Antonio Stars

My Best Day was when my son was born!

-KIKI VAN DE WEGHE

NBA Small Forward, Denver Nuggets, Portland Trail Blazer, NY Knicks. LA Clippers, Coach: NY Nets, 2X All-Star, UCLA Basketball 1st Team All-Pac 10, NBA Executive Vice President, Basketball Operations

"The Shot" in 1998 was my Best Day! My brother, Bryce Drew had the game winning shot against Ole Miss with 2.5 seconds left on the clock to advance to the Sweet Sixteen.

-SCOTT DREW

Basketball Coach, Valparaiso, Baylor, 2013 NIT Championship

My Best Day was when I got traded to the Celtics. The Players, The Boston Garden, The Management, The Championship.

-HANK FINKEL

LA Lakers, San Diego Rockets, Boston Celtics, 1974 NBA Champions

My "Best Day in Pro Basketball" came in Los Angeles at the Fabulous LA Forum, when my Team (Boston Celtics) won the 1968/1969 NBA Championship.

My Grammar School gym teacher here in Chicago had retired and was living in LA. I gave him my tickets to all four games of the Championship Series played there in LA.

After the game he came down to the court and we embraced and cried joyously. That was the last time I saw him and a memory I carry with me all the time.

-EMMETTE BRYANT

NBA point guard; NY Knicks, Boston Celtics, 1969 NBA Championship

My Best Day in football was this year's CIF Championship game vs. Villa Park at Anaheim Stadium. We won that game 28-10 for my First C.I.F. Championship as a Head Coach. I lost in the finals in 2001, 2006, and 2009. I was calling myself the Marv Levy of high school. Looking back I really respect Coach Levy for getting to four straight Super Bowls. My players really wanted to win that game for me and that touched me greatly. All three of my sons were on the sidelines during the game & that was quite special. Matt '04 & Hunter '07 played for me at Edison and each lost in a C.I.F. Final game- Matt '01 and Hunter '06. Garrett is a 9th grader at Edison and hopefully he will get a chance to play in a final game one time

-DAVE WHITE
Football Coach, Edison High School

Yesterday was the Best Day of my life. I get to marry the girl of my dreams.

-KYLE CALDWELL

Setter-UCLA Volleyball, All American Honors

The Best Day I've had in my life up to this day would have to be in the summer of 2013. I went to Laguna Beach with my best friend and girlfriend, and spent the whole day laying on the beach and swimming in the beautiful ocean. Then to top it off, going to my house that overlooks the bay and wish every day that I could do it all over again.

Also, winning the 2014 and 2015 NCAA Championship at Loyola back-to-back.

-CODY CALDWELL
2014 & 2015 MVP NCAA Championship, Loyola University at Chicago Volleyball.

Every day I wake up is my Best Day! I see life as a great adventure & I enjoy and appreciate every spectacular moment that is given to me.

-GAIL GOESTENKORS

Head Basketball Coach, University of Texas

I struggle to select one day from a lifetime of blessings. My Best Basketball Day was coaching the 2008 Olympic Women's Basketball Team to a gold medal. What made this day "better" than other Olympic Golds I had been fortunate to be a part of was my brothers and sisters; all 7 (one is spirit) were in China to share that time with me. The bond of family, the extreme support they showed, and our deep love for one another made the gold medal the most priceless memory I have.

-ANNE DONOVAN

Head Basketball Coach, East Carolina, Philadelphia Rage, Seattle Storm, Seton Hall, Connecticut Suns, 2004 WNBA Champion, Olympic Basketball Coach; Olympic Gold 1984 LA- 1988 Seoul-2004 Athens-2008 Beijing

If it is pertaining to Sports, from the Bull Pen to pitch in Yankee Stadium. I had 2 outs and 2 runners on base, Mr. Mantle was the batter. 60 thousand in the stands. I got him to strike out!

-BILL LEE

MLB Pitcher, Boston Red Sox, Montreal Expos, 1973 All Star

My Best Day is hard to narrow down. Everyday I wake up and my family is healthy are great days. But I will narrow it down to winning a gold medal in Australia. It wasn't just winning, but all the years of sacrifice from time spent with family and friends, to all the time physically spent preparing. It also feels good when you set a goal for yourself and attain it not all by yourself but with all the people who have influenced and touched my career. So, the pride of representing my hometown, University and USA!

-KATE SMITH

Basketball Player, Minnesota Lynx, Detroit Shock, Washington Mystics, Seattle Storm, 3X Gold Medalist in 2000 Sydney-2004 Athens-2008 Beijing, 2X WNBA Champion, 7X WNBA All-Star, 2001 WNBA scoring champion, Women's Basketball Hall of Fame

Second to my marriage to my wife, Nancy, of 55 years, the Best Day would be winning the PGA Championship in 1964. It opened many doors in my golfing career and gave me a lifetime exemption on the tour.

-BOBBY NICHOLS

Professional Golfer, 12-time PGA winner, 1964 PGA Champion

I've been blessed to have many Best Days. I married a beautiful
woman (25 years and counting) and have four incredible
children.

The Best Day ever was the day by autistic son Matthew
graduated from high school. High school was hard for matt. My
wife and I cried with joy as we watched him walk across the
stage to accept his diploma.
The next Best Day ever will be when he graduates.

-STEVE DONAHUE

*Head Basketball Coach; Cornell, Boston College, Penn, 4X Ivy League
Championships, 2X NABC District Coach of the Year, 2018 Ivy League Coach
of the Year*

I know my father's "Best Days" are right now. He was the best father anyone could wish for. He has all my awards, and I know there are rewards for that. Good luck with your book.

-JOHNNY LOGAN

As told by his son, John Logan Jr.

Boston/ Milwaukee Brewers, Pittsburgh Pirates, 1957 World Series, 4X All-Star

Bumping down a narrow dirt road, the cab let my sister and I, plus some fellow UCLA friends out in front of a group of children. Six cute little pumpkin heads brought us to a small house surrounded by pineapple fields. This would be my home for 3 months while I studied Spanish and travelled the beaches of stunning Costa Rica. As I watched the salmon sky fade to dark, I watched my Costa Rican family picked fresh pineapple for juice, and tucked me into bed in the master bedroom. As simple and as pure as this day unfolded, all I could think about as I lay my head to sleep in this amazing little home in the amazing little rain forest, is that the love this family has is far greater than any accolade or UCLA award I've ever experienced. That was love!

-KIMBERLY COLEMAN
UCLA Setter, Coach, Harbor Day School

Enjoy this "Best Day"- I had in winning the 1955 U.S. Open.

-JACK FLECK

US Golfer, 7 Professional wins, 1955 US Open Winner

I would have to say that my Best Days are any that I get to spend with my two daughters and wife doing some kind of activity and hanging out. I realize that's not specific, but it really is what I look forward to any time I am able. It also helps if it's a sunny beach day…

-RICCI LUYTIES

1988 Seoul Olympic Gold Medalist, UCSD Head Coach Women's Volleyball

Ah, the Perfect Day   .

The day of my greatest happiness is if I am on my ranch
on a Sunday afternoon and all are sitting at the same table. My
six grandchildren and my six children and my lovely wife are
sitting at the same table. That would be the ultimate.

-GARY PLAYER

*Professional Golfer; Golf Hall of Fame, 3 Master wins, 1955 US Open
Winner, PGA Winner 1962 & 1972*

My Best Day really has nothing to do with basketball, you see my son at age 14 (skinny waisted broad shoulder basketball player) was in a horrific wake board accident. He was life airlifted to a hospital, on life support for four days after a brain surgery to remove half the side of his skull and stop the bleeding in his brain, he was in intensive care for 11 days. We took him to TIRR in Houston, when we entered that facility he could not walk, talk, hold a fork in his right hand, and he was drooling out of the left side of his mouth. Within seven days he walked unassisted down the hallway and 28 days late he walked out of there like nothing ever happened to him, so I just shared two of the best days of my life, the day he walked and the day he walked out of TIRR. Ironically nine months later, as the Associate Head Coach my team at Texas A&M wins the National Championship in women's college basketball, there is a picture of me on my knees giving God the glory as the horn sounds.

-VIC SCHAEFER

Women's Basketball Head Coach, Mississippi State, Texas A & M

I had two successive "Best Days" when I was fourteen years old. On Friday, May 13, 1955, I was hitchhiking in Ridgecrest, California. A guy picked me up and talked me into going to church that night. They were having a youth rally. The speaker was a "fire and brimstone" kinda guy. God spoke to me and I received Jesus Christ as my Savior. That is the best day a person can have—forgiveness of sin and the promise of eternity with God.

The next day they had a youth retreat and since I was a new youth in the church I went. A girl that I had been noticing at school came over to me and introduced herself. At 6'3" and 136 pounds, I was super shy. She was 5'10" and weighed 110 pounds. I thought she was perfect. We had a great time together and she invited me to her birthday party the following Friday. She was three months older and was turning fifteen. We have been together ever since. We dated for seven years and got married when we were twenty-one. At this writing, we have been and item for sixty years.

I met my savior and my mate in two successive days. They were the Best Days of my life.

-JAY CARTY

NBA Power Forward, LA Lakers

Happiest day- every day! I enjoy everything I do and everyone I meet.

-TARA VANDERVEER

Basketball Player, Indiana, Head Basketball Coach, Ohio, Stanford University, 1995-1996 Olympic Team

What was my Best Day? That is a question that I could answer differently at different times in my life. I'm fortunate that I've got a lot of options to choose from and each holds a special place in my heart and mind.

When I was a teen, I might've told you it was winning a high school state championship or earning a college scholarship. Early in my 30s, I might've told you it was leading the University of Maryland to the 2006 National Championship in woman's basketball. That one will always rand right up there with the very best. And in a way, that plays into my evolution as a person and leader.

As I get older, it seems like the best days of my life are more other people. My greatest happiness now comes from seeing people I love smile. That day in 2006 was certainly one in which I was surrounded by smiles and a group of people achieving their dreams. And it's easy to understand why- we beat rival Duke in a dramatic overtime finish. Just four years earlier, in my first year at Maryland, they drilled us by 51 points.

However, just two years after coaching Maryland to that National Championship, my husband and I became parents to twin boys, our first children. Bringing new life into the world in an experience nothing else can ever compare to. It's the greatest form of happiness anyone can ever know.

Since that time, our children have brought smiles to our faces seemingly every day. They've also taught us so much about life and why we need to stop racing around and appreciate the present moment.

What stopped us in our tracks was learning one of our sons had cancer. The doctor's diagnosis was leukemia and it brought my husband and I to tears. We entered the world of oncology, a place we never planned on visiting. Over the more than three years of chemotherapy we met amazing people and learned about life in a way that we otherwise might not have. We are fortunate that our son's prognosis is very good, and it seems like his story will have a happy ending.

So, when I look back on what was the Best Day of my life, I can say it was the day our children were born. It made me a better and more balanced person in ways I couldn't have understood at the time. And, oh yeah, while I was in the hospital delivering twins, my Maryland team beat Duke again.

-BRENDA FRESE

Head Women's Basketball Coach, Ball State, Minnesota, Maryland, 2006 NCAA National Championship, 2002 AP Coach of the Year, 2X Big Ten Coach of the Year

First thing, I was lucky enough to play for the best college basketball coach ever, Pete Newell. In case you didn't know, we beat UCLA eight straight times when I was at Cal. As a player being on the National Championship team in 1959 was great. The next year, the 1959-1960 season I started and had some good games. First, I guarded Jerry West in the 1st L.A. Classic and held him to 8 points. His lowest in his college career. Then I guarded Oscar Robertson who was averaging 35 points a game. I held him to 18 points in the NCAA semi-final game. A big disappointment came the next night when we lost to Ohio State. We finished 28-2.

As a coach the teams I had at Corona Del Mar were great and the players as well. I had a great time at the get togethers seeing those guys. Winning the State Championship in 1979 at Orange Coast College with local guys was the highlight of my career in coaching.

-TANDY GILLIS

Basketball Player, University of California, National Championship 1958-59 season, Head Coach, Corona Del Mar High School, Head Coach, Orange Coast College, 1979 State Champions

What must have been my Best Day is now missing from my memory. I had extensive memory loss but most of it has come back—but no NASCAR racing in 1988. I won my third Dayton 500 in 1988 at age 50 with the best young driver second, my son Davey. Four months later I crashed at Pocono and had severe head injuries as well as many broken bones and other injuries. The head injury was nearly fatal. After 19 years and a lot of help from my wife Judy, and family and friends I have recovered quite well. I just have no memory of Daytona '88. I do remember a party Sunday night at Parks Seafood Restaurant in Daytona Beach (still one of my favorite places to eat!).

-BOBBY ALLISON

Race Car Driver; 1971-1973,1980-1983 Winston Cup Most Popular Driver, NASCAR Hall of Fame, International Hall of Fame of America

My basketball Best Day was in the Elite Eight in 1999 when we lost to Connecticut 67-62. Interesting that my best day was a loss at Gonzaga, but we were so close to the Final Four. My only regret is that it was so early in my career. Now I would appreciate the experience so much more!

-DAN MONSON

Head Basketball Coach, Gonzaga University, Minnesota, Long Beach State

On a personal note, "My Best Day" would be the day I married my wife of 59 years. She has always been my strongest supporter and has enjoyed being a football coach's wife in every way. She has only missed 4 games in the 59 years and those were due to family births and death.

On a professional note, "My Best Day" would have to be the day I was hired as football coach/athletic director in Summerville High School on July 1, 1952. Summerville was a football town when we came here and had remained one throughout the years. We were a very small school and town in 1952, but over the years, we grew to be the largest high school in South Carolina. Then we were split into two more high schools. However, our talent pool remained constant throughout the changes. I've been blessed with good talent, great community support, and a lot of luck.

As for milestones, there have been many during the 60 seasons- when I broke Gordon Wood's (of Texas) record for the most wins nationally (406) in 1993 and when I reached the 500 number in 2003. I have been greatly blessed in many ways and feel very lucky to have reached the number of 590 wins at 85. I hope to continue working as long as I am physically and mentally well.

-JOHN MCKISSICK
Head Coach, Summerville High School

It is hard to choose just one, but I decided my Best Day was probably the day my son, Matt, was born on December 17, 1991. Winning the Winston a few weeks ago was a close second.

-MARK MARTIN

Race Car Driver

My Best Day in football occurred in 1962 when I tied an NFL game record with seven touchdown passes. I fired pass after pass to such star receivers as Del Shofner, Frank Gifford, Joe Walton, and Joe Morrison. My backs protected me too. Usually a quarterbacks' uniform is smeared with dirt and grass stains, but my blue jersey and gray pants were virtually spotless. My blockers gave me the time to complete 27 of 39 passes for a total of 505 yards and all the Giant touchdowns in a 49-34 victory over the Washington Redskins.

-Y.A. TITTLE

Quarterback; Baltimore Colts, San Francisco 49ers, New York Giants, 7X Pro Bowl, 4X 1st team All Pro, 3X NFL passing touchdown leader, SF Hall of Fame, NY Giant Ring of Honor, Pro Football Hall of Fame

My Best Day as a pro football player was during my first season in 1984 with the Indianapolis Colts, after the third preseason game. I was wearing jersey number 48. Jersey number 48 and playing linebacker was a good sign. So, after the third game of the preseason against the Seattle Seahawks I was awarded jersey number 56 because of my play against the Seattle Seahawks. With the new jersey number 56 came a spot on the 50-man roster. I had made the team as an undrafted player. That was a date to be very proud of and I was.

-VERNON MAXWELL

Linebacker; Indianapolis Colts, Detroit Lions, Seattle Seahawks, 1983 NFL Defensive Rookie of the Year

I have two Best Days:
1) The day I recognized the preference of God, my wife and I embraced Him.
2) The day I met my wife, Jamie, which changed my life and was a life saver.

Everything else pales in comparison.

-DICK STOCKTON

Sportscaster, American Football, Baseball, Basketball

For most athletes, the "Best Day" probably comes from some personal achievement of a championship win and honors afterward. I have to admit to growing up in a large family of outstanding athletes" Patty: basketball. Softball in the 1960's; Tom: football, tennis in the 1960's; Mark: football, basketball, scholarship to Cal, Cathy: cheerleader, Ann: every sport a natural in the 1970's and 1980's; mostly decorated for basketball, Jeff: basketball, baseball; Susie: swimming, Kelly: softball, basketball; Colleen: track, and Bobby" tennis…you can see that the Meyers family had a deep love for sports based activities that were supported by Bob and Pat Meyers- our athletic parents.

So, being #5 in a family of 11, I was following older siblings with many accomplishments. Thus, my senior year at Sonora High School in 1970-71 I quietly became a better basketball player by working out with my brother Mark during the summer. At the start of practice a few weeks into the beginning of my senior year I broke my ring finger and had to have it re-broken to avoid season ending surgery. I started rehab, and I only missed 6 games. Our team was 5-8 when we started league and we ran off 14 straight wins to win the CIF 2A Championship with Paul Bush as our innovative coach. So the Best Day was our CIF semi-final game playing Maraleste, who was the Number 1 seed. That night I was playing well in the 1st half, we were up by 10 and I received 2 technical fouls within two minutes of each other. I thought high school was like the NBA, so I just walked off the court thinking I was ejected! (Bad Day- I just ruined the year). The ref came and told Coach Bush, "One more word out of #35 and he's gone." Well, I went from worst (I didn't play until the 2nd half again and in the 3rd quarter basically kept my mouth shut but played tentatively) to the best with our team coming from behind and the passing of our guards Tim Hoston and Brad Hillman, to our big guys and we won a stunning upset of the #1 seed. My emotions were so precarious it was hard to get my self-control back after the final buzzer. That game was a microcosm of my year from worst feeling to great feeling and it mirrored my emotions in that one game. The next week was anti-climactic beating El Centro by 9 for the Championship.

I have played in many historic games at UCLA for Coach Wooden, however; none ever matched that year at Sonora. Even in the NBA I played against some great players and with marvelous athletes in Milwaukee but never had the deep imprint of that semi-final game in High School.

With my career of course, Coach Wooden was the "Best 4 Years", I couldn't have scripted that part of my life any better. The relationship, the deep impression he had made on me and my whole family has been life altering. Yes,

I've had many tremendous "Best Day" in sports but I will savor that one in 1971.

As for "My Best Day in Life", getting married in 1975, the birth of our daughter Crystal, then the 1979 birth of our son, Sean were great days. I have been able to be home with the upbringing of our children, help my neighbors in the community to make life changes through God's word, and keep my life simple from the "keeping up with the Jones" mentality. So, I appreciate each day we have to help others and spread the wonderful Kingdom Hope Jesus taught about.

-DAVE MEYERS

Power Forward, UCLA Basketball, NBA Milwaukee Bucks, 2X NCAA Champion, 1975 1st team All-American

My Best Day is each day or the present day. At my age, you can understand.

-LOU SABAN
Linebacker / Placekicker Cleveland Browns, NFL Head Coach; Buffalo Bills, Denver Broncos, Head Coach, Northwestern, Maryland, Army, 2X AFL Champion, 2X AFL Coach of the Year, Buffalo Bills Wall of Fame,

My Best Day by far was the day that I put Christ 1st in my life and became a Christian! September 10, 1983!

-LORENZO ROMAR

NBA Point Guard; Golden State Warriors, Milwaukee Bucks, Detroit Pistons, Head Basketball Coach, Pepperdine University, Saint Louis, University of Washington., 2X Pac-12 regular season champion, 3X Pac-12 Coach of the Year

My Best Day is a tie:
1) Wedding Day- everyone is bias, but our wedding was the best- a 3-day holiday weekend celebration with our families from New York and Michigan coming together for a great weekend in Syracuse; where Deb and I went to college.

2) The June day when we closed on our first house in the morning and got engaged right after that.

-MIKE TIRICO
Sports Announcer, ESPN, NBC Sports, Play-by-Play Notre Dame,

329

My Best Day was the day my 1st child was born…my Best Day professionally was the win in Super Bowl XXXI.

-MIKE MORNHINWEG

NFL Coach; Green Bay Packers, San Francisco 49ers, Philadelphia Eagles, NY Jets, Baltimore Ravens, Head Coach Detroit Lions, 2010 NFL Assistant Coach of the Year.

My winning run for gold in the Olympic Downhill was the Best Day of my life!

-ANTONIO DENERIAZ
Skier; Olympic Gold Medal 2006 Turin

As far as my Best Day goes, there isn't one particular day that stands out as my best. I believe that every day has the potential of being your Best Day. The day that I married Robin, the days that my three children were born, and winning the SCCA Trans-Am Championship two years in a row stand out among many occasions.

I think I still have Best Days to come. For instance, when I win my first NASCAR Winston Cup race, or win my first Winston Cup Championship.

-WALLY DALLENBACH JR

Professional Race Car Driver, Racing Announcer,

My Best Day at UCLA Volleyball was in January 2011 when we played #1 ranked USC in Pauley Pavilion. UCLA had thousands of fans in attendance and the place was loud. I ended up getting 14 kills on 18 attempts, this game really started my successful career at UCLA.

-WESTON DUNALP

Quick Hitter, UCLA Volleyball, 2012 2nd team AVCA All-American, 1st team All-MPSF

My true answer to your question is "everyday" that the Lord allows me to wake up, be around a great group of people, and coach football is my BEST Day! Everyday is a new beginning.

If I have to be specific, then my BEST day as a coach would be when we won the ACC Title for the first time in 20 years.

-DABO SWINNEY
Assistant Football Coach, Alabama, Head Coach Clemson, 2X National Championship, 6 ACC Division Titles, 3X Paul "Bear" Bryant Award, 2X ACC Coach of the Year

My Best Day is easily recalled. It is the day that I was inducted into the NFL Hall of Fame. I say this not because of the honor itself, which is very overwhelming, but because of the attending circumstances. At the time, I was coaching for the Steelers and, of course, the induction weekend takes place in the middle of training camp practices. Therefore, I had to ask permission to be absent from this very busy portion of the NFL's year.

To my great joy and forever unending gratitude, the Head Coach, Mike Tomlin, and the Rooney Family owners not only agreed to my absence, but arranged for the entire team to be present in Canton, Ohio the day I was inducted.

I will never forget being able to look over at their section and seeing the entire Pittsburg Steeler organization sitting there.

To share that moment with them and my family- well, that for sure was MY BEST DAY.

-DICK LE BEAU

Cornerback / Safety; Cleveland Browns, Detroit Lions, 3X Pro Bowl, 3X 2nd Team All-Pro; NFL Coach, Philadelphia Eagles, Green Bay Packers, Cincinnati Bengals, Pittsburg Steelers, 2X Super Bowl Champion, 2008 Sporting News Coordinator of the Year, Pro Football Hall of Fame

My Best Day- Football:
My interception for a 53-yard touchdown return. I can still hear
the band playing, "it's alright now" and it was!

-STEVE FOLEY
Defensive Back, Stanford University, NHHS Football & Track Star

My Best Day: The Los Angeles Lakers first victory parade in 2000, downtown LA was just the Staples Center and a lot of parking lots. I was covering the parade, when Shaq saw me running along side of the cavalcade. Shaq stops the bus- and said "you, The Brick-come on board". I rode the bus with Derek Fisher in back of the bus with millions of screaming fans. The ultimate bliss.

-VIC "THE BRICK" JACOBS
Radio & TV Announcer

My Best Day is every day I awake from a deep sleep is my Best Day.

-KENNY EASLEY
Strong Safety, Seattle Seahawks, 5X Pro Bowl, 4X 1st team All-Pro, 1984 NFL Defensive Player of the Year, Pro Football Hall of Fame, College Football Hall of Fame (UCLA)

My first job was at Brea Olinda High School where I was fired as the head "varsity" basketball coach and "B" basketball coach with no assistants. Who else would have taken this assignment but an eager newly college graduate?

Brea had not done much in football for many years, so expectations were not very high. We were a school of students in 4 grades. We had about thirty boys out for football. Certainly, a great moment for me was our last game with Laguna Beach on their field. We were 3-4 going into the game while Laguna was undefeated and heavily favored. We won when no one gave us a chance. This was the first big thrill as a head coach. We started winning the next year, and eleven years later, when I left for Orange Coach College, we had won 97 games with 8 Championships and 2 CIF titles with lots of thrills. We had great kids who played in those eleven years. We had three CIF players of the year. I doubt any other school had three.

I went to OCC in the fall of 1962. Coast had been down for a few years, so it was a good time to start. With an overwhelming freshman team, we went 9-1, which was the most wins in one season ever. We went to a bowl game with most everyone back the following year.

In 1963 we were undefeated and selected to play in the Junior Rose Bowl in Pasadena with over 44,000 fans in attendance, a National TV audience and all the celebration that went with this event. We beat the number one ranked team in the nation, 21-0/ Chick Hern, the famous sports announcer, called the game. We shut out six teams and ended up #1 in the Nation.

We also had a great year in 1975 when we were undefeated and ranked #1 in the nation. That team did not have a close game and was truly a great team. A big bonus was having my son Rhett on this team as a linebacker.

Another highlight in my career was the year I retired from football at Coast. In 1986 I coached a team in Finland and took my son Clay, a quarterback. We had a great time and played in the Finnish Super Bowl. Clay was picked as the Player of the Year while I was picked as the Coach of the Year. It was a fun experience.

We won 5 Championships in my years at Orange Coast College, but I would have to say the 1963 experience, with all it entailed, would be my greatest thrill!!

I had a wonderful time coaching football those thirty-five years. Those people I worked with, the players and assistant coaches were all talented and fine people to be associated with.

Wish I could do it again.

-DICK TUCKER
Head Football Coach, OCC, 4X Conference Titles, 1963 National Champions, Orange County Sports Hall of Fame,

I was competing at the Arcadia Track Invitational in my high school senior year and was recruited by Sherry Calvert, a three-time Olympian javelin thrower. At the time, she was the head women's track coach and assistant volleyball coach at USC. I was recruited for two sports; high jumping for track and indoor volleyball.

My junior year, there were many good days at school, the busy life of a student/athlete included sports, classes, the bustle of students scurrying here and there to fulfill their daily schedules, prominent professors sharing their extensive knowledge, top notch coaches training their athletes to the best of their ability…pretty incredible as I reminisce of the past. I was a member of the 1976 and 1977 Volleyball National Championship teams. Also competed in the Track Nationals my sophomore and junior years. I was surrounded by a plethora of top athletes, many who continued their athletic careers at a professional level, as did I. Yet, this one day stands out more than most, simply because I was so grateful for the outcome of that day. It was not one of athletic prowess, but more of mental and physical strength and perseverance.

I was walking home from track practice, at the end of my junior year, to my apartment one block off campus across from 32nd Street Market. It was dusk, pretty dark with the cars' headlights shining and the streetlights illuminating the sidewalk in front of me. This was my routine and route since I was a sophomore, with no problems to date. As I was walking, I noticed a VW Bug, to my left, driving in traffic. I didn't think anything of it. I turned right, into my apartment. The door led straight to the stairway or elevator, which took you up to the first floor of apartments. I usually chose the stairs, quicker and more exercise. I reached the top of the stairs and began opening the door. I heard someone running up behind me. I thought I would be kind and hold the door open for them to go first because they seemed to be in a hurry. At this point, I hadn't seen who it was, simply heard the running footsteps getting closer. It was a black man, not much older than myself. I couldn't tell you what his features were like, it all happened so quickly and certainly unexpectedly. Instead of walking through the door, he stopped, wrapped his strong hands around my throat and began choking me. Of course, I was very surprised since my mind was still focused on offering an act of kindness to another person (opening the door for him). My mind was struggling to make the shift to the act of violence and cruelty that was happening. It was almost like watching a horror movie except instead of watching the screen, you were the main character on the screen. Being confronted with this situation and never being mentally prepared, you have no prior knowledge as to how you should respond/defend yourself. I couldn't answer his questions because he was cutting off my air supply completely. He asked where was my money? Did I have any money? He tightened his grip, squeezing and squeezing until everything went black, I finally passed out. As I came to, I was at the bottom of the cold, stone staircase. He had descended the stairs and was standing there, looking down at me. I was understandably dazed. I always wondered why he hadn't taken my bag and ran while I was unconscious. My educated guess is that he thought he had killed me and wasn't sure what to do. He recognized I was gaining consciousness, grabbed my workout bag containing my clothes from practice and my purse. He turned to leave. I asked, "Please don't take my bag, just take the money." He actually stopped, handed me my bag and told me to get the money out. I found my wallet and he grabbed it from my hand. Again, I pleaded, "Please don't take my wallet, it has all my ID's, just take the money." He handed my wallet back to me and told me to get the money. As I extended my hand with the money, he asked, "Is that all you have?" It was $18.00. My response, "I'm an athlete on scholarship. My family has no money." He stood me up, since my leg hurt and had difficulty standing, and walked me back up the stairs. It felt as though there was a gun or knife held against my back, but to this day, I don't know if there was or wasn't. In situations such as these, we could beat ourselves up thinking we could have done different or more. I tried very hard to not do that to myself. I figured it was enough to just let it go. I wasn't willing to take a chance and try to get away. Next, he told me to take my pants off. I asked, "Why?"

The response being, "I don't want you to run after me." I replied, "I can not walk, let alone run!" As he began to undo my pants, I could hear the door opening below. Someone else was entering the stairwell, the perpetrator heard it too. He opened the door into the first-floor apartment hallway and disappeared as the door swung closed behind him. One of the students who lived on the first floor, ascended the stairs. He saw me standing there and asked if I was OK. My mind was foggy, my body was in shock and my adrenaline was racing. I responded by giving a short scenario of the event and requested him to stay with me a minute or two to allow the guy to get away. I wasn't sure if he was armed or not, but didn't want to take the chance of my neighbor getting injured. We waited, then entered the hallway to find it empty.

The finger I wore my high school class ring on, was almost severed. It must have caught on one of the stone stairs as I tumbled to the bottom, unconscious. I began to shake as I rummaged through my bag for my keys to the apartment, noticeable signs of shock. At the time, I was good friends with Randy Simmrin, who had been a wide receiver for the USC football team, graduated the prior year. I called him asking if he could come over, I needed his help. He asked what was up and was I OK. I told him I'd share what had happened when he got there. I didn't want him getting upset and getting hurt on his way over. He drove me, what seemed a lifetime, to find an open emergency room. It took us three tries before we were able to find medical assistance. They tended to my finger and asked if anything else hurt. I shared that I was sore from the fall, but I would be alright. In hind sight, they didn't check for a concussion and they took no x-rays. They had to cut the ring off my finger. I kept the ring and still have it this day. Forty years later, it resides on my left, pinky finger. I didn't report the incident to the police. I couldn't say who it was or what he looked like. My thoughts are that he was being jumped into a gang and it was something he was told to do. He was in the V.W. Bug with other guys who followed me to my apartment.

I did report the incident to the trainers at USC. They checked me over, but no x-rays were taken. Years later, I was playing racquetball and broke my big toe on the cement wall. In those x-rays, the doctor mentioned how terribly my broken ankle had healed. We argued, or rather I argued with him insisting I had never broken my ankle. He showed me the image, then the light bulb went on…an ah ha moment, all the pain through the years. I was relieved that it all finally made sense. I wasn't crazy. I've always had a very high tolerance to pain and this one I couldn't block out. I had been running and jumping on it all summer. Fall season came around for my senior year. My ankle hurt so much that I made the difficult choice not to compete in volleyball and try to focus solely on track/high jumping. Pre-season jumping was painful, but made no sense to me since it wasn't my take off leg for jumping. The doctor at USC took no x-rays, but rather gave me a cortisone shot instead. We did hot and cold treatment, ultrasound, but nothing seemed to ease the pain. It didn't make sense to my coach, Sherry, either. I know, throughout the years, she thought I was a quitter. I missed volleyball, but the head coach, Chuck Erbe, was a touch coach pushing us through intense workouts. I was doing two-a-days, volleyball and track all year round. I knew the pounding of the hard wood volleyball courts would end my athletic career. Little did I know, it was already ended. It was devastating to me. I knew there had to be a reason for the pain, but the experts didn't find it…they didn't look. I had to stop doing what I loved and what my entire life had been about. No volleyball my senior year and stopped track halfway through the year. Most of my teammates never knew about the incident. I never wanted to talk about it. I wouldn't even let my parents come see me. I told them I was OK. I told them they didn't have to take the trip out to school. Volleyball coach never knew, he just thought I quit. Years later I shared with my track coach, Sherry. I felt I needed her to know that I truly am not a quitter. I began as an athlete at

USC at the age of 17 and graduated at 21. I trusted my life and wellness to the professionals. My thoughts were, I'll do the sports and classes, you just look after me. As the Universe would have it, I wasn't to continue sports at the time. It wasn't in the stars for me. Fifteen years later, I returned to competition by playing professional sand volleyball for five years.

My best day was when I woke up at the bottom of the stairs, knowing I lived to see another day…to add more chapters to my book of life.

-JULIA LENDL-CELOTTO
USC Track & Field, Volleyball

My Best Day in football was coaching my two sons on Championship Teams seven years apart. I know it was tough on them but it sure was special for me. It also made mom, Anita, happy!

-JOHN BARNES

Coach Los Alamitos High School, The winningest coach in Orange County History

My Best Day could have been when I won my first Gold Medal at the Tokyo Olympics. It was an event that no one including my Olympic Coach thought that I had a chance. My best events were the 200 & 400 freestyle (which I hold the World Record) and most people thought I would also swim in the 1500. When I decided no to try the 1500 meter and went for the 100-meter sprint people thought that I was nuts, but I wanted to try. When I finished 1st in the finals it was a thrilling moment for me. I was so excited that I almost didn't make it to the victory stand in time (I was only 18 years old).

Or my Best Day could have been when I carried the American Flag into the Olympic Stadium for the closing ceremonies. I was proud to be an American and proud to be the one who represented the entire USA team.

Or it could have been the day I graduated from Yale University. When I didn't go to a swimming college after the Tokyo Olympics (like USC, Texas or Indiana) most people again thought I was nuts. But I wanted to see if I could compete in a tough academic environment in a small school. The day I graduated with a BA in Economics was to me as big as achievement as my gold medals.

Or my Best Day could have been the day each of my three children (2 boys & 1 girl) were born. The happiness that I experienced on each day was different than my happiness which I felt in my personal success. This happiness was shared with my wife and was full of future expectation not past hard work. The fact that all three kids were healthy was an added bonus.

No, my Best Day was seeing my middle child, Kyle accomplished something I had always dreamed of doing. He played in the State of Oregon 6A (high school) football finals championship.

When I was growing up, I heard all of the stories of my father playing football in North Dakota. He was a high school All-State halfback. Then when my older brother got to high school, he too became a high school All-State tackle in Oregon. My dream was to do the same but to go one step further- to go to the State Finals.

I never got the chance because by the time I entered high school I was already breaking records in swimming. Although I won two races at the State Championship my freshman year, and our high school won the State Title, and it wasn't in football.

I stayed with swimming, but I always regretted that I wasn't able to accomplish my football dream. Then when one of my sons did it, and I sat in the stands at the University of Oregon and watched that championship game; it was my Best Day of my life. (Kyle's team didn't win-they lost in the final 5 minutes) But, Kyle could say he was there, and I was there to see it.

I have been fortunate to be blessed with many good days in my life.

-DON SCHOLLANDER
Olympic Swimmer, 4X Gold Medalist Tokyo, 1 Gold, 1 Silver Mexico City

About the Author:

Mark Keys is a Southern California native, residing in Costa Mesa with his wife Laurie, daughters, Page and Megan, their dog, Fumble, and five cats, Lucy, Ethel, Sammy, Frank & Jack-Jack.
Mark loves that his mom still lives at the beach in Newport in the house he grew up in, and he spends a lot of time there with her & the girls; and loves walking the beach. He played basketball growing up, in High School, and beyond; as well as body surfed until he injured his back. Mark is an avid reader, enjoys watching classic movies & westerns, collecting film and sports memorabilia, walking and listening to Jazz, Motown, and Rat Pack music. He also loves to travel and going to sporting events & team practices; when health permits. In spite of his numerous surgeries, including 6 back, 13 ankle, 1 neck, 3 shoulder, and 14 knee surgeries (plus 4 knee replacements). H also experienced shingles, pneumonia, MRSA Staph infection, he has no immune system and fights continuous migraines and other health issues every day. But, through all of this, he keeps a positive attitude and outlook to make each day, his best day.

Made in the USA
San Bernardino, CA
08 January 2020